I0185728

Listening for Lies

HEARING THE DIFFERENCE BETWEEN THE SPIRITS OF THIS
WORLD AND THE HOLY SPIRIT, AND WHY IT MATTERS.

SHANA PELTZ

Design by Sophia (Jilek) Larson
Published by: Shana Peltz

ISBN: 979-8-9905353-1-2

Dedications

TO MY READERS,

I wrote this book as an act of obedience to Jesus. I am kicking fear in the face and surrendering the outcome to God. My prayer is that this book will provide support to individuals who may be experiencing similar struggles as I have. While I can't say that I had a desire to share my journey and failures, I believe that God is urging me to step into deep waters. I am placing my trust in Him to guide me through. Even if I stumble in this earthly life, I find comfort in knowing that my success lies in eternity, so I set my eyes upon that ultimate goal. And I encourage you to do the same!

TO MY BELOVED CHILDREN,

This book is for you. It serves as my heartfelt attempt to share my life's journey with you as honestly as possible. I acknowledge that words alone cannot fully capture the complexity of my flawed existence, but I have tried to do my best. Throughout my life, I've made choices I regret, and my hope is that as you read these pages and listen to the depths of my heart, you will glean wisdom from my missteps. Never forget that God's love for you is immeasurable. It is imperative that we continually reach out to Him. His compassionate hand is always within reach, patiently waiting for your invitation. He is a gentle presence who respects our free will and awaits our permission to intervene in our lives.

TO MY TREASURED BOYS,

I am so proud of each of you! Words cannot express my love for you. I urge you to embody the qualities of a true gentleman. Become men who prioritize their love for Jesus above all else. Stand firm and courageous in your convictions, for this is an incredibly appealing trait. Let your actions honor and uplift others, and humbly pursue your goals. Remember, society will contradict our values, but it is crucial to maintain clarity in both your mind and heart, enabling you to discern the Truth. Navigating through these complexities can feel impossible at times but I promise, you have what it takes! Stand strong, bravely do the right thing. Embrace your role as men of character, guided by the light of Jesus' love and you WILL be a success.

TO MY PRECIOUS DAUGHTER,

You are the missing piece of my life that God knew I needed the most. Through your presence, you have taught me more than I could hope to teach you. Despite my shortcomings in expressing it, I hope you have always felt the depths of my love for you. Please know that I am a work in progress, constantly striving to become better. Never allow the world to tell you who you should be, that is a job only for God. And he says you are a masterpiece, uniquely designed and not meant to conform to anyone else's expectations. Your creator has extraordinary plans for you! He desires to give you wings so you can soar! Place your trust in Him, keep your eyes looking forward and he will guide every step. Our emotions can deceive us, but God remains our unchanging source of Truth. Keep your mind rooted in His Word, fix your heart upon Him, and everything else in life will fall perfectly into place.

TO MY LOVING HUSBAND,

You are a gift that I know I don't deserve. Isn't it just like Jesus to exceed our hopes and give more than we can imagine? You have surpassed all my expectations as a man and a partner. Countless times, I have stood in awe of the immense blessings God has bestowed upon me through you. Among fathers, you rise above them all. Your love for us knows no bounds. The way you selflessly give your time and energy to our family is unparalleled. Just witnessing your dedication exhausts me in the best possible way. I cannot express enough gratitude for everything you are to us. I think I'll keep you!

MY TREASURED FAMILY AND FRIENDS,

You are a desire of my heart and having you in my life is truly a dream come true. I am in awe of how God has graciously given you to me. My fervent prayer is that I have faithfully nurtured this precious gift, inspiring and guiding you to become the individuals God has destined you to be as well. Thank you for helping me grow, trusting me with your love, and making life on this earth a blast! The love I have for you surpasses what words can express, and I am immensely grateful that we will spend eternity together.

TO MY FELLOW AUDIO READERS,

Having spent countless hours immersed in the world of audiobooks, I feel a deep connection with you. May this book serve as a source of inspiration as you engage in daily tasks like washing dishes, folding clothes, or driving around town. I want to acknowledge the sacredness of your work, as you carry out God's holy purpose in your daily lives. May you be abundantly blessed for your faithful efforts.

With all my love,

Your mom, wife, and friend

-Shana

Table of Contents

Is the Bible true?

Hey! If you are thinking about skipping this part, please don't! It's an important part of the book even though it's not a chapter. ;)

If you're like me, you're asking "why make it the prologue if it's so important! Why not a chapter?" If this is you, we understand each other! Welcome to my tribe and thank you for picking up my story.

In order to maximize the benefits of this book, it is crucial to establish a strong foundation. Just like all great houses are built upon a solid base, I cannot expect you to trust my words blindly. I am human, just like you, and I make mistakes on a daily basis. Consequently, there is nothing I can say that possesses eternal value because, similar to you, I am simply striving to navigate this life to the best of my abilities. My hope is to learn from the mistakes I make along the way, but **I have a secret weapon.**

Well, okay, I suppose it's not that much of a secret, but I do like to add some dramatic flair! I have been fortunate enough to possess a tool that has consistently proven its worth in my life. This invaluable tool encompasses eternal wisdom and guides individuals towards a fulfilling existence. This book is the Bible, and the hero of the story is Jesus. The Bible contains a multitude of life stories, encompassing both successes and failures, along with rules and guidelines for living. Above all, it shares the remarkable story of a man who came to heal our wounded hearts.

It is an undeniable truth that life has a way of breaking us. I have personally experienced countless moments where I found myself utterly shattered, with my heart in pieces. However, in those moments, God has consistently come to my rescue. He has lovingly repaired my broken heart and not only restored my joy, but also blessed me beyond my wildest imagination. Even when I didn't have love for myself, He loved me unconditionally. He waited patiently for me during the times when I turned my back on Him. Through His example, He has taught me how to love both others and myself. And most importantly, He has loved me enough to grant me the freedom to choose whether I will trust Him each and every day.

The Bible serves as the foundation of my imperfect and some-times messy journey. As I reflect upon my past and the numerous flawed choices I have made, I realize that if only I had followed its instructions, I could have spared myself from so much pain. However, I am someone who often learns the hard way. Particularly during my younger years, I felt the need to navigate life on my own terms. If that sounds like you, then we understand each other.

Fortunately, unlike any other person in my life, God exhibited unwavering patience when I walked away from Him. There was no shame, no disapproving glares, and no harsh words. He simply waited. He allowed me to have my own way and patiently awaited my return, knowing that I would eventually seek His guidance and assistance. He never imposed Himself upon me or made demands. He simply waited. And I want you to know that He is waiting for you too, with the same unwavering patience and love.

Each of us enters this world from unique corners, brought up in diverse families with distinct values and life experiences. I acknowledge that much of what I share may not align with your personal story, as it is likely different. However, my heartfelt prayer is that God will utilize my story to aid in the healing of your own. We have the capacity to learn from one another's life experiences and apply them to our own circumstances. While joining hands, we can support each other in discovering who God has called us to become. Together, we can navigate the challenging and uncertain path ahead, ultimately finding ourselves firmly positioned within God's perfect plan for our lives.

Life is undeniably challenging, and oftentimes, we inadvertently contribute to its complexity. Our actions and choices can further complicate an already messy existence. We often believe that forging our own path will lead to personal fulfillment and happiness. However, I have come to realize that pursuing our own way typically results in two outcomes: a life filled with relentless struggles and perpetual disappointment. Constructing a "good life" highway is not our forte; our roads are plagued with potholes and sharp turns. This is precisely why we are in dire need of an owner's manual! The Bible has endured the test of time for various reasons, one being that it works! The lessons it imparts, the practical applications it offers, and the Person it leads us to follow have all been tried and proven to be divine Truth.

In my own life, the only lasting success I have ever had was when I followed Jesus's Word. This kind of success is offered to anyone willing to put in the work. And yes, it is work. All good things come from great effort (and we'll get to that more later in the book).

I could spend a significant amount of time explaining the infallibility of the Bible, its prophecies, the proven stories, and the consistency it has maintained over thousands of years. However, I believe that the discovery of this Truth is a personal journey that each individual must undertake. I have faith that the Holy Spirit will guide your heart to find belief as well.

My healing and joy have been made possible through the Word of God and the guidance of His Holy Spirit. Living a life aligned with His law is not without challenges, but the rewards are immeasurable. **You** are valuable beyond measure. **You** are capable of more than you realize. And most importantly, the Creator of all things loves you deeply, and that love will lead you to unimaginable places. All that is required of you is a willing heart. You must believe and trust that His words are true. Doubt can lead us astray, but trust opens up a world of possibilities. Will there be battles? Certainly, but we have the ultimate guidebook on how to emerge **victorious**.

So going forward, when I quote scripture, try not to skim through it. Don't switch off your brain or daydream. This is the time to really focus. Eliminate any distractions. Remind yourself that this is the **great** stuff! It's a perfect battle plan for my life! It's the creme de la creme!

I love you and thank you for taking this journey with me.

CHAPTER ONE:

Count The Cost

"Satan promises the best, but pays with the worst;
he promises honor, and pays with disgrace;
he promises pleasure, and pays with pain;
he promises profit, and pays with loss;
he promises life, and pays with death."
- Nancy Leigh DeMoss

I haven't always been so passionate about spiritual awareness and discerning lies. So, first, let me share how I reached this point. I first had to fall into a pit of deception, then as the blinders were peeled away, I looked around to see my folly. I gripped the sides of the rocky soil and bit by bit climbed out of the pit before arriving here. It's astonishing, even to me, how a girl raised in a nurturing, loving household became an expert in succumbing to the lies within my own mind. Despite being bruised and battered, I fought my way out, and now, as a woman, I am determined to empower others to shake off the dust, tend to their wounds, and embrace the life that God intended for them!

Being a bit rebellious was part of my nature. It wasn't the kind of rebellion that led to frustrating adults or landing me in jail, but rather a quiet undercurrent of defiance. Obedience, submission, and adhering to rules always seemed to rub me the wrong way. And let's face it, rules can be dull and restrictive. Don't get me wrong, I strive to be a good person who loves Jesus and treats others with kindness, but as I was transitioning into adulthood, I found myself yearning to do things my own way. I'm the type of person who needs to explore and figure things out on my own. I've never quite grasped how people could simply trust their elders and obediently follow the rules. It seemed incredibly boring to me, igniting my curiosity even further! Besides, wasn't Jesus a rebel himself? He challenged the norms of his time and lived on the edge! Okay, I admit it might be a stretch to compare my disobedience to that of Jesus, but I think that he understands me.

From a young age, a war raged in my mind between right and wrong, good and evil. I yearned to live life on my own terms, doing things my way. However, I also had a deep love for God. Throughout my teenage years, I found myself in a constant battle: loving God while resisting submission, loving God while struggling to walk in obedience, and loving God despite my aversion to authority. As you can imagine, living a Christian life has been far from easy. My strong desire to figure things out independently has come at a great cost, but I have also experienced tremendous forgiveness. This book tells my story, including all the messy and ugly parts. However, more importantly, it explores God's incredible transformative power. It demonstrates how trusting in God's ways not only brings redemption to all things, but also leads to an abundant outpouring of blessings.

* This book is intended for the person who has made mistakes, perhaps too many to count.

* This book is for the person who wrestles with doubts about the goodness of God.

* This book is for the person who is ready to confront and challenge the lies they have embraced.

* This book is for the person who needs a gentle nudge in the right direction.

* Above all, this book is for YOU, because God has placed you on this earth, in this time, for a unique purpose, and there is no one else quite like you. The path you have chosen holds significance and is meant to help others who share your struggles and experiences.

Our future starts with what's happening in our minds today. There is nothing we do in life without thinking about it first. So why do we still make so many poor choices? The best and the worst of us fall for the lies of the enemy. And there isn't a person on this earth who is exempt. Satan knows he cannot outright attack God and expect us to go along with it - he must be subtle! He understands that he must appeal to our desires and twist the truth... just a little. His deception appeals to our natural human desires. He starts small, hoping we will agree without even noticing his quiet whisper. He starts with doubt, just like Eve in the garden.

Satan started with a woman. Now, I don't believe this is because women are weak or naive. I believe he attacked women first because he knows how much we bring to the table! Women are world-changers. One life at a time, we hold the potential to affect the world around us. Women are a powerful force, making a difference in our homes, workplaces, and communities. If Satan attacks us and suc-ceeds, he knows he will bring down many more with one blow. This realization should ignite a fire within all of us to put on our armor and defeat him!

Our minds are a bustling place, teeming with activity. Each day, we generate thoughts and make decisions based on those thoughts, which ultimately determine the path we will take. Life is brimming with choices. Will we rise early or succumb to sleeping in? Will we respond with a "yes" or a "no"? Will we exercise our bodies or opt for the comfort of the couch? Will we engage our minds or mindlessly scroll through screens? Every day, we possess the power to steer our lives in a direction that either improves or worsens our well-being. However, while the choices may seem solely within our control, I also acknowledge that it's not always as straightforward as it appears.

It is crucial to recognize that every choice we make comes with consequences. Nothing in life is free, and God, out of His love for us, grants us the freedom to choose our own paths. Understanding this is paramount. God will not intervene to prevent us from ruining our lives because He loves us deeply and respects our autonomy. Some individuals opt for smoother paths, while others, like myself, seem to require the lessons learned from bumpy roads. We may find ourselves on detours that take us the long way around, incurring significant costs, but hopefully, we can find our way back. Even when my poor choices came with steep price tags, I understood that I was responsible for the outcomes. I did not place blame on God when the consequences of my actions came crashing down; I held myself responsible.

However, later in this book, I will talk about the time when I did blame God. I truly felt God let me down. I fervently asked and believed in healing for my dying mother and this is when feelings of anger began to take hold within me. I didn't feel that my request was too much to ask. After all, He performed miracles countless times in the Bible. Why wouldn't He do the same for me?! Where was my miracle?! I'm sure many of you have found yourselves asking God the same question at some point or multiple points in your lives.

Every choice we make carries a cost

But when it comes to our choices, the cost is high, regardless of whether we opt for a safe or daring approach. We all desire a fulfilling life, but greatness does not come without a price. Here's the good news: We have the privilege of selecting what we want to pursue, be it great things or easy things, the longer, more challenging path or the quick shortcut. Every choice we make carries a cost. **Nothing** is truly free! It's essential to carefully consider the price and continue moving forward. This vast and wondrous life has an abundance to offer, and the power of choice is in our hands.

* Doing the right thing is hard. Doing the wrong thing is hard.
* Earning money is hard. Being broke is hard.
* Finding good friends is hard. Living with lousy ones is hard.
* Getting healthy is hard. But being unhealthy is also hard.
* Saving yourself for one person is hard. Losing yourself to many is hard.
* Trusting God is hard. Trusting the world is hard.

Do you see the pattern? Life = cost. Nothing is free. It's crucial to imprint this truth in the forefront of our minds. Every choice we make comes with a price tag. Each thought we entertain inspires a decision, and each path we choose becomes an investment in our destination. I hope that this sobering reality does not instill fear, as fear bears no fruit. But rather, use this truth to get back on the path of a beautiful, healthy life! We all experience failures at times, but ultimately, we can surrender those failures to God. Here lies the incredible part: He can handle our mistakes better than anyone else, certainly better than I have managed to handle them. Only He possesses the ability to transform ashes into beauty. Only God has the power to turn our blunders into masterpieces. It is my hope that this book will guide you toward discovering your own masterpiece.

MY FIRST ENCOUNTER WITH THE ENEMY

From a very young age, I had a strong awareness of God's presence in my life. However, I also experienced a profound pull towards evil. I grew up in a modest house with a compact kitchen and six people crammed inside. It may have been small, but it was our home. I remember the comforting scent of Mom's cooking wafting through the air, while Dad diligently studied for his college degree at the table. Meanwhile, I would find myself lost in daydreams of kicking Satan's butt, engaging in literal battles with him right in our living room. I would raise my fists in the air, picturing Satan on the opposite side, and I would throw punches and kicks until I was breathless. Naturally, I always won. Even as an eight-year-old, scrawny armed kid, I threw a strong punch. ;)

I adored my house, with one exception: the basement bathroom. It was tucked away in a dark hallway that perpetually felt damp and cold. The only thing nearby was the even darker and damper storage room where my dad loaded shotgun shells. My bedroom, on the other hand, was located upstairs, close to my parents, while the basement was reserved for my teenage siblings (and ghosts). One night, I was pulled out of my sleep and unconsciously walked down to the place I dreaded the most within our home: down the long, shadowy hallway and into the musty basement bathroom. I abruptly awoke, startled to find myself standing in front of the dimly lit mirror, gazing at my own reflection. My eyes widened, and a wave of panic engulfed me. I felt trapped as an audible voice repeated over and over again, **"I'm going to get you... I'm going to get you..."** Fully awake now, I was seized by immense fear. I knew deep within my being that this was a demonic spirit directly taunting me! It was different from a dream; it lacked the same confusion or curiosity that accompanies a dream. I recognized it immediately. This spirit was aware of my vulnerabilities as a child and exploited them. But why? Why had it singled me out? As soon as I could gather my trembling legs, I sprinted upstairs as fast as I could. Breathless, I collapsed onto my bed and, with wide-open eyes, I prayed earnestly, "Lord, please protect me! Don't allow those spirits to enter my home ever again. Guide me and help me. Satan will not have his way!" I continued to pray until my eyelids grew heavy and my body relaxed, eventually allowing me to drift back to sleep.

This experience awakened a deep realization within me from a very early age. I embraced the idea that I was being sought after by two opposing forces: good and evil. And the reality is, we all are! Both God and Satan are actively at work every single day. God's influence is gentle and loving. Satan speaks lies while hiding the truth. He uses both pleasure and pain to deceive us.

"Be alert and of sober mind. Your enemy the devil prowls around like a roaring lion looking for someone to devour."

1 PETER 5:8

Without comprehending this fact, it becomes challenging to perceive life for what it truly is: a constant interplay of spiritual forces operating behind the scenes, vying for our attention. It is crucial that we take responsibility for whom we choose to serve through our actions. The book of Joshua says it best, "Choose this day whom you will serve." Rest assured, we are all serving someone (or something).

Which voice is the loudest in our lives? Unfortunately, too many times in my life, it was the deceiver's voice that was loudest in my ear.

In the years that followed, I found myself making numerous poor choices. I would often justify and deceive myself, convincing myself that these decisions weren't as detrimental as they appeared. Deep down, however, I knew that they were not in my best interest. Still, I felt the need to navigate this journey on my own. Through my mistakes, Satan sought to instill fear and doubt within me. And for a season, he succeeded. He aimed to undermine my faith in God. And for a season, he achieved that too. He desired for shame and guilt to be the final verdict in my story. Yet, I found my way back, guided by the Holy Spirit's unwavering Truth that countered those lies. My pains and failures served as reminders that only God possesses the power to heal all things. Within my heart, I crafted a declaration: "I belong to God, and I am here for a purpose!" I recognized that I have something valuable to offer this world. This mindset became an investment in my healing journey and a proclamation that would transform my pain into triumph. God knew that I desperately needed this resolve because there were still countless failures awaiting me ahead.

Which voice is the loudest in our lives?

Through the renewal of our minds, we can experience transformation.

In the first chapter, we embark on our first action plan: acknowledging that nothing in life comes free, everything carries a cost, and our future begins in our thoughts. Ultimately, we have the power to choose the price we are willing to pay. However, I understand that it's not as straightforward as it may seem. Life becomes intricate and complex. Our thoughts, dreams, and desires often entangle us, influencing the decisions we make. Additionally, our fears and failures unconsciously shape our choices. Yet, with dedicated effort, we can begin to perceive things for what they truly are. Through the renewal of our minds, we can experience transformation. We will gain a heightened awareness of the impact each decision holds in our lives, and we will step into the purposeful life that God has ordained for us. This path may not be easy and it may involve hardships, but it is a road adorned with heavenly peace.

"You keep him in perfect peace whose mind is stayed on you, because he trusts in you."

ISAIAH 26:3-4

This road we tread is not only a path towards transformation but also a journey of healing our wounded hearts and discovering how to embrace joy amidst pain. I urge you, no matter the circumstances, to never give up. You have successfully completed chapter one, and I assure you that living the life you were destined for is absolutely worth the effort. So, let us join hands and embark on this road together, supporting and encouraging one another every step of the way.

REFLECTION QUESTION

What kinds of ideas are filling your mind these days?

Have you ever considered the fact that there are spiritual forces operating behind the scenes, vying for our attention? Have you ever felt these forces pulling you in one direction or the other? Explain.

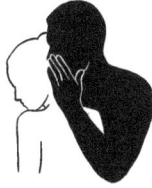

CHAPTER TWO:

Whispers

"If you want the truth to go round the world you must hire an express train to pull it; but if you want a lie to go round the world it will fly; it is as light as a feather, and a breath will carry it."
-Charles Spurgeon

PART 1: LYING WHISPERS

It starts with a whisper. It's that voice in our minds that affirms what we believe is true and discredits the things we don't. It's a voice that feels and sounds like our own. But what if that whisper in your mind is not only your own but rather, it comes from another realm? What if the spirits of this world are also speaking to us, whispering ideas, thoughts, and dreams into our mind?

Have you ever considered that there is a spiritual world aiming to win you over? These spirits are working overtime to sway you into actions and beliefs.

In 1 Kings 22:21-22 these spirits accomplished just that. There were over 400 prophets who unknowingly gave Ahab, an evil King, counsel that came directly from lying spirits. Let me be even more straightforward. A demon, remaining invisible, transferred his ideas into the prophets' minds. The Bible gives no indication that these prophets had any idea that they were being led by a lying spirit. And since all 400 had the same counsel for Ahab, he believed it to be good advice! Not to mention, and of equal importance, it was the advice Ahab wanted to hear!

It says "Finally, a spirit came forward, stood before the Lord and said, "I will entice him.""By what means?" the Lord asked. "I will go out and be a deceiving spirit in the mouths of all his prophets,' he said.

Whether we acknowledge it or not, we are continuously influenced by one of two voices (whispers, if you will). Our thoughts are not always our own and it is crucial for us to learn to discern these voices if we want to make decisions that align with God's plan for our lives.

During my teenage years, I didn't realize the battle that was happening for my soul. I didn't understand that my thoughts were not always my own. And I was blinded to the extent of authority I had unwittingly given to Satan. That's the hard truth. **He can take nothing from us without our consent.**

"Submit yourself to God. Resist the devil and he will flee from you!"

JAMES 4:7

I am not saying that all the bad things that happen to us are our own fault. We live in a world full of corruption, so it's inevitable that bad things happen to many good people due to the amount of evil in the world. What I am saying is that at some point in my youth, I had to first crack open the door. I opened the door just enough for him to slip his slimy finger inside. Once that happened, it became very difficult to close it again. When a door is opened, you find yourself fighting an uphill battle, which is exactly what I did. I gave my consent, agreeing with the whispers and collaborating one little choice at a time. Without even realizing it, I handed over the keys to take things that I truly cherished. It wasn't until much later and after shedding many tears, that I discovered how quickly and quietly this had happened.

I grew up in a healthy home. My parents treated each other with love, and I never feared they would get a divorce. They worked hard and provided us with everything we needed. As a child, I remember my father working all day and studying at night as he made his way through college. My mother was also a hard worker. She hadn't taken a sick day from work in 30 years. She had a kind and soft-spoken nature but could be tough as nails when necessary. She prayed aloud all the time, often kneeling beside her bed, constantly engaging in conversation with God. She had a unique intuition, as if Heaven confided in her and shared its secrets. She was the kind of mom that boyfriends were intimidated by, and rightfully so.

Growing up, we attended church at least three times a week. I actively participated in my youth group, leading worship, hosting Bible studies at my home, and taking part in church talent competitions. I was fully committed to living out the teachings of the Bible, and my love for Jesus was unwavering. I enthusiastically invited everyone from school to join me at my youth group on Wednesday nights, even though I faced ridicule for being a "church girl." Surprisingly, the negative comments didn't bother me; in fact, they fueled me and strengthened my resolve. My bold and confident personality earned me the admiration and high regard of my youth leaders and pastors.

During this time, my mother also began her battle with a rare skin disease and later cancer. This disease caused constant itching and burning sensations all over her body, which persisted day and night. As a result, she experienced fatigue, frustration, and constant agitation. Unfortunately, due to the rarity of the disease, the doctors were uncertain how to effectively treat it. They resorted to using medications to alleviate the symptoms, leading to a countertop filled with numerous pill bottles. Despite her condition, my mother never stopped working full-time, volunteering at church, and attending all my athletic and music events.

It was during this difficult time that I introduced a new boyfriend to my parents, whom my mother did not approve. He was popular, well-dressed, and had a way of making me feel incredibly special whenever we were together. He attended church with me, enjoyed watching rom-cons, and took me on unforgettable dates. What set him apart was his indifference towards what others thought of him dating the "church girl." In my eyes, he was perfect. However, my mother held a different perspective. She saw something that I couldn't see at the time, and her disapproval greatly offended me (leading to the first whisper). I felt she was being narrow-minded and controlling (whisper). It seemed as though she was disconnected from my life and unwilling to give him a fair chance (whisper).

And so, my relationship with my mother quickly deteriorated and became strained. With each push from my mother, I pushed back even harder. Before long, our home became a battleground, not just for her disease, but also for control over my relationship. It was a relentless war between us. In my youthful arrogance, I believed I knew better than my mother (whisper). I saw her as old-fashioned and clueless about what was best for me (whisper). On the other hand, she firmly believed I was making a huge mistake, and I became adamant that she was wrong. In fact, I could handle myself (whisper). During this tumultuous period, I made a silent agreement within myself, listening to the whispers that affirmed what I already chose to believe. I allowed my emotions to guide me, convinced that I knew what was truly good for me and that I could handle the choices I was making (whisper). **These seemingly simple decisions set the trajectory for the rest of my high school experience.**

I overestimated the power within myself while underestimating the power of the deceiver.

One evening, my boyfriend and I dressed up for a wedding that we attended with our friends. To be honest, I wasn't even sure who was getting married—I was simply the '+1'. At the reception, our group of friends sat together, passing around a plastic beer cup, with everyone taking swigs except for me. Drinking was something I had never done before, and I had no desire to try it. My boyfriend, however, had a history filled with stories of girls, alcohol, and wild experiences that my innocent mind didn't want to know. Nevertheless, he was slowly finding his faith in Jesus, and I understood that redemption is a process. I was content with the pace at which he was changing. After all, he had already made so many sacrifices for me, so a few sips of beer didn't seem like a big deal.

After the wedding, we headed to a friend's house. Although our friend was out of town, he had given us the key, allowing us to hang out at his place if we wanted to. It seemed like an exciting idea— an opportunity to have some fun. We wouldn't have to worry about interruptions, and we could enjoy a little alone time before heading home. We made our way downstairs to our friend's bedroom, where we laid on the bed, laughing and kissing. My boyfriend had an intoxicating presence. His confidence and cool demeanor made me feel secure and exhilarated. Moreover, he possessed a special kindness and tenderness that set him apart. When he looked at me, it felt as if I were the most incredible person in the world. In his arms, I melted away, and his every move felt perfect... until it wasn't.

As more clothes were removed, I began to feel a sense of losing control, unable to find an escape from the situation I had willingly entered. My initial excitement quickly transformed into confusion and frustration, as I realized how far things had escalated. My mind was spinning, overwhelmed with everything that was taking place. And amidst the chaos, I experienced a sharp and painful sensation while I struggled to understand what was happening. Fear gripped me, adding to the mounting emotions. Yet, I lacked the courage to speak up. I felt a sense of stupidity for being so naive, and I didn't want to appear foolish by asking, "What's going on? What is happening?" However, it didn't take long for me to understand the situation. I lay there, as confusion, fear, and shame took hold of me. When the pain became unbearable, I finally mustered the courage to speak, pleading, "Why does it hurt so much? Please stop." And with those words, it was over. My heart sank, and my dreams for the future were shattered. A profound sadness consumed me.

As we drove home that night, I gazed out the window, silent tears streaming down my face. My thoughts were consumed by self-condemning words: "This is all my fault. I am so stupid. I am a fraud." (whispers)

While the whispers of shame and self-loathing were deafening, these were not the whispers that got me here. The crack in the door opened long before I even realized it. The foundation was laid before I even realized my alignment. The whispers that got me here were the quiet ones that felt like my own. "I know what's best and my mother is out of touch." THOSE are the ones that led me to hand my consent to the enemy. These tiny whispers in my mind appealed to my desires, making it easy to open that door.

And when those lies were exposed, as they inevitably are, Satan replaced them with new ones- louder ones! This time, however, it wasn't just a finger in the door; he forcefully held it wide open, using shame as a doorstop. Satan is cunning and perceptive. He intensifies his efforts when we are vulnerable and weakened, tirelessly working to deceive and lead us astray.

THE NEW WHISPERS TOLD ME:

* That was all my fault-(lie).
* I am so stupid-(lie).
* I am not good anymore-(lie).
* Nobody else will want me-(lie).

And so, with the doorstop in place, and lies settled deep in my heart, I continued on this path.

PART 2. WHISPERS OF TRUTH

It always starts with a whisper. Just a crack in the door.

Whether we are aware of it or not, there are numerous voices that influence our thoughts and emotions throughout the day. It is crucial for us to take control of this inner dialogue and not allow our thoughts to dictate our actions. The Bible has a lot to say about this actually.

"We demolish arguments and every pretension that sets itself up against the knowledge of God, and we take captive every thought to make it obedient to Christ."

2 CORINTHIANS 10:5

Many times, our thoughts are influenced by our feelings, but feelings themselves are not reliable. It is risky to allow our emotions to dictate our actions, as they are often based on personal experiences rather than objective truth. In the specific situation leading up to the night I lost my virginity, I genuinely believed that I was capable of handling it. My emotions assured me that we were in agreement and that I had no reason to be concerned. Similarly, my feelings convinced me that my mother was mistaken and lacked understanding. However, it became evident that those emotions were deceptive and untrue.

Firstly, we need to identify whether our thoughts are rooted in feelings or truth. It is significant that the Bible mentions the word "truth" over 225 times! In John 8:32 Jesus said, "you will know the Truth and the Truth will set you free." This verse highlights two important aspects. Firstly, the "Truth" referred to here is the written words of God, the Bible. This is the reason I always put a capital T. Secondly, the Creator of the universe, the God who brought everything into existence, grants even someone as insignificant as myself the ability to comprehend His Truth! It is astounding to consider this. In a world saturated with falsehoods vying for our attention, we have the opportunity to have the blinders removed from our eyes and perceive the world in a manner that only God's people can. We can grasp concepts that originate directly from the Almighty Maker of heaven and earth. This is not just any truth; it is THE Truth! And it is accessible to us; we simply need to seek it!

> *"If any of you lacks wisdom, you should ask God, who gives generously to all without finding fault, and it will be given to you."*
>
> **JAMES 1:5**

There is another thing that God gives His people; conviction. Conviction arises when we commit ourselves to the authority of God's Word, construct specific beliefs based on our understanding of His Word, and have the courage to act upon those beliefs. Conviction serves as a guiding force, leading us towards the Truth found in

God's Word. It is the only divine Truth that can align our feelings with right thinking and right living.

This is truly wonderful news! In fact, it is the best news! Why would anyone choose to dwell in confusion amidst the lies of the world, being swayed back and forth by every worldly idea, when they can approach the Creator of all things and have a clear understanding of what is actually true?! Easier said than done, I know. The voices of this world are loud, and it can often be challenging to discern which voices are influencing our lives, particularly when we lack a strong foundation in the Truth of God's Word. However, finding clarity is possible! God is a God of clarity, not confusion. He desires us to have clear minds that can discern our feelings and grasp the Truth. We don't have to remain in a state of confusion.

During my youth, while I received valuable Biblical teachings, the concept of the spiritual battle we face on a daily basis was not explicitly discussed, or perhaps I wasn't receptive to understanding it. I held the belief that my thoughts belonged solely to me, and likewise, my actions were solely my own. I remained unaware of the invisible forces at work, influencing and shaping my thoughts and actions from behind the scenes. And from the first moment I acted out my disobedience towards my mother, I gave way for negative spiritual forces to take ground in my life. We always make that choice on our own! The big, bad devil can take nothing without our consent. We must always remember that. It's also important

Conviction serves as a guiding force, leading us towards the Truth found in God's Word.

to remember that though the spiritual world is busy working overtime to pull us in the directions they want us to go, God gives His people enormous authority and spiritual awareness, we need only to ASK for wisdom! The hard truth is that often, in our immaturity, we don't want to do the right or good thing. We want the easy road. We want the road with immediate gratification. So it takes tremendous bravery to listen and obey God. **His ways are not our own!** But He loves us so much that when we ask, He will always tell us the hard Truths.

Let me go back to 1 Kings and the story about Ahab listening to the counsel of the 400 prophets. There is more to this story! There was one prophet, Micaiah, and he didn't give the King the same counsel all the others did. While the others said, "Yes, go to war! You will win!" Micaiah said, "If you go- you will die." This wasn't what the king wanted to hear. He became angry and threw Micaiah in prison. This same principle holds true for us today. We ask for God's help, sometimes we even seek a godly person's counsel, and when we don't like the advice given, we lock it away much like what the king did to Micaiah. Because oftentimes, godly Truths don't sit well with us. We would rather choose the counsel that feeds our ego or aligns with our will. God's Truths do neither, they are the hardest to obey, but they are **always** the best!

But why? Why is listening to godly counsel so difficult? Let's go back to our beginnings. Let's go back to where this all started. **The Bible tells us: We are born sinful.** "Therefore just as sin came into the world through one man, and death through sin, and so death spread to all men because all sinned" Romans 5:12

Without God's help, we simply aren't adept at making good decisions. We lack a track record of consistently making good choices. What's even more unfortunate is that we are born with a natural bend towards wrongdoing. Every single one of us is affected by this inclination. And to further complicate matters...

God gave Satan power over earth. "You used to live in sin, just like the rest of the world, obeying the devil-the commander of the powers in the unseen world. He is the spirit at work in the hearts of those who refuse to obey God." Eph 2:2 This scripture indeed reveals that Satan is actively at work in the hearts of humanity. His intention is to lead people towards making poor choices. However, it is important to note that his tactics are not obvious or easily discernible. Satan is known as The Great Deceiver for a reason. The choices and ideas he presents will often be wrapped in enticing packaging. They may appear good or even great on the surface, appealing to our personal desires.

So we find ourselves in a double challenge. Firstly, we were born with an inclination to do wrong, and secondly, Satan is actively working to deceive us. With these factors at play, it is evident that there is a loud voice in our lives vying for our attention. However, the Bible also teaches us about God's still small voice, as mentioned in 1 Kings 19:11-13: "...and after the fire, a still small voice..." I encourage you to read the entire story sometime, as it is truly remarkable. Despite the powerful events occurring—wind, earthquake, and fire—God was not in those manifestations. In other translations, it describes His presence as "the sound of a low whisper." This perspective offers valuable insight. When we are discerning between these two voices, it becomes clear which voice is the loudest.

HOW DO WE ACCOMPLISH THAT?

Listening is indeed a skill that can be developed and strengthened over time, much like a muscle. Just as we need to put in dedicated effort and time to build stronger muscles, the same applies to honing our listening and perceiving abilities. The exciting part is that there are practical actions we can incorporate into our daily lives to cultivate a keen and discerning ear.

If we seek to listen to God's voice, we must silence the other and patiently await the whisper.

It begins with reading the Bible. Hearing and recognizing God's voice starts with immersing ourselves in His written Word. Just as in any relationship, communication is key. We become acquainted with a person's mannerisms, values, and even the sound of their voice over the phone. This principle holds true for our relationship with God as well. We need to invest time in getting to know Him. In doing so, when life bombards us with lies, as it often does multiple times a day, we can swiftly identify them based on the truths revealed in God's Word.

"My sheep hear my voice, and I know them, and they follow me."

JOHN 10:27

But that's not all! This daily practice of reading your Bible will bring so much more. It will provide you with God's wisdom and power.

"He gives power to the weak and strength to the powerless."

ISAIAH 40:29

"For the Lord gives wisdom, from His mouth comes knowledge and understanding."

PROVERBS 2:6

Wisdom, power, knowledge, and understanding. Wow, don't we all desire these qualities? We often believe that the world can offer them, but true wisdom, power, knowledge, and understanding can **only** be found in the creator of these attributes. (You should read that last sentence again.)

Which voices are you attuned to? If you are unsure, take a moment to reflect. How well do you know Jesus? Are you regularly reading

His word and asking for wisdom? To what extent do you follow His teachings? If you have doubts or uncertainties, it may shed light on the answer to the initial question.

As I contemplate that night from my youth, it feels incredibly surreal that I couldn't grasp what was happening in that moment. How did I, a good Christian girl, find myself in a bedroom with my clothes off? Why did I appear so confused? Was it due to denial? Was I so naive? Or was it because I had listened to the lies that were whispered along the way? I believe the answer to all these questions is yes. It all began with the lie I convinced myself of, that my mother didn't understand me. Furthermore, my inner rebellion led me to insist on doing things my own way. I genuinely believed that I knew what was in my best interest.

After that night, failure was etched onto my heart. I hadn't yet realized that these voices were deceitful; they resonated with me as though they were truths. I had unintentionally opened the door, although just a crack, allowing him to slither into my mind so discreetly that I remained unaware of his presence. I assumed complete responsibility for all my failures, accepting them as my own burden, and consequently believed that I must keep them concealed and locked away. What would people think if they found out?! Exposure will ruin me. (more whispers) So, with that, I locked the door and threw away the key.

Oftentimes, we overestimate the power within ourselves while we underestimate the power of the deceiver.

And sadly, this wouldn't be my last time.

Take some time to evaluate your own inner dialog.

What are you hearing? *

What are your thoughts telling you about yourself or others?

How are those thoughts affecting your actions?

CHAPTER THREE:

The Heart is a Liar

"Well, I think we tried very hard not to be overconfident, because when you get overconfident, that's when something snaps up and bites you."
- Neil Armstrong

I overestimated the power of myself while underestimating the power of the deceiver. The overestimation of oneself is not uncommon. We all experience it at some points in life. Our brain convinces us that we are experts in our own lives. We believe that we know ourselves best and therefore understand what's best for us. Perhaps, as I say this, you might agree. Yes, I am the authority on my own life. And in certain ways, this is true! We do possess the most knowledge about ourselves compared to anyone else. We are the only ones who hear our thoughts and comprehend our motives. However, when it comes to being an expert in living our lives, that is where we deceive ourselves. Our circumstances shape us, and our upbringing molds us. Yet, none of that grants us expert status on how to live successfully. Often, we are guided by our emotions and life experiences, following our hearts. Society encourages us to "follow your heart," but the Bible presents a different perspective in Jeremiah 17:9, stating, "The heart is deceitful above all things and beyond cure." So, which is it?

The Bible references the heart over 800 times, and while we typically associate the heart with the physical organ that sustains life, the Bible speaks of the heart in a different sense. It acknowledges that the heart holds wisdom, makes sense of the world, experiences emotions, and makes choices. It serves as a filter, influencing and directing our thoughts, actions, and interactions in both work and play. Every thought originates in the heart, which often leads to action, extending from the internal to the external. Additionally, our heart absorbs our experiences, acting as a storage container. It utilizes these experiences to guide our actions. In the context of the Bible, the heart encompasses much more than a physical organ; it serves as the conduit through which our mind, soul, and spirit are influenced. Ultimately, the heart is the center of our emotions. Considering this, it becomes crucial to submit our hearts to Truth and place them under God's authority. If left under our own control, our hearts will be unable to attain the wisdom and authority they were designed for. And though I'm not talking about the muscle that pumps blood, I firmly believe that our lives depend on it.

Every thought originates in the heart, which often leads to action, extending from the internal to the external.

"I will give them an undivided heart and put a new spirit in them. I will remove from them their heart of stone and give them a heart of flesh."

EZEKIEL 11:14-21

This passage reveals that with God's assistance, we can receive a heart shaped by His divine influence. He will instill a new godly spirit within us and revive our lifeless hearts, but when left in our control, mistakes are bound to happen. Our hearts, without God's guidance, do not lead us to the Truth. Instead, they often deceive us by telling us what we want to hear. And often, it is a lie. Let me explain.

When I reflect on my youth, I realize that my heart often dictated my actions, as is common for many people. Despite having knowledge of what is Truth, my heart would pull me in a different direction, one that felt good and appealed to my desires and emotions. Even though I had grown up learning about what was biblically right and wrong, the world presented me with enticing offerings that felt right to my heart. I wanted to believe that what my heart was selling me was true. I was willing to take the risk because, in my mind, it seemed like a small deviation from the right path, a mere click off course.

This is where our downfall begins. I don't mean to sound overly dramatic, but let's face it: most people don't simply jump off a cliff. Instead, we inch closer to the edge, cautiously peering over, stepping back, and repeating this process until we gather the courage to take the plunge. Similarly, when we veer off course in life, it usually happens gradually. We mistakenly assume that evil will manifest as an obvious figure with red horns and a cape. We expect to see it coming in a clear and recognizable form. However, that is not how Satan operates. He is subtle and crafty, twisting God's Truth ever so slightly and presenting it in a way that looks and feels good, leading us astray with just a slight deviation (a little click) off God's path. He may also take God's truth, pose a question, and plant doubt in our minds. This is the reality of evil. It always begins subtly, aligning with our heart's desires.

Leading up to the night I lost my purity, everything my heart was telling me seemed rational. The heart possesses an innate ability to appear trustworthy and persuasive. It creates a sense of certainty within us and feels inherently right. Sadly, the gentle and unwavering voice of Truth stood little chance against the multitude of competing influences that were shaping my life during that time. Honestly, I didn't even pause to seek God's perspective. And the underlying fact is that I didn't want to know what He thought. Deep down, I was already aware of His thoughts. I knew what I desired, and I was determined to heed the voice of my heart because it brought me pleasure and satisfaction in the moment. I was reluctant to embrace the unknown that awaited me on the other side of placing my trust in God.

Trusting God is indeed challenging for us. It goes against our natural inclination. Despite knowing that He alone possesses complete knowledge of the past, present, and future, and acknowledging that He is the creator and perfecter of all things, we still struggle to trust Him fully. This struggle often reflects my own lack of genuine belief in God's goodness and His plans for my life. I find myself doubting His goodness and fearing that if I seek His direction, it will contradict my desires. I worry that God will remove things from my life instead of adding to it. Letting go of control is a difficult and frightening endeavor. Therefore, I neglected to pause and ask for His guidance, continuing to stray further from my intended path. I chose to listen to my heart rather than engaging my rational thinking, and as a result, that initial small deviation grew into a significant distance from my original course. My heart led the way, setting me up for failure. I unknowingly walked into a trap of my own creation, blinded by its existence. This is precisely why the heart is so deceptive.

My heart received the information, that information was stored, and new actions began to pump out of that experience. The heart holds it all.

"Above all else, guard your heart, for everything you do flows from it."

PROVERBS 4:23

A few more things changed for me that night. Firstly, a seed of deep shame was planted within me. I felt ashamed for giving a part of myself that I had sworn I never would, not until I was married to the right man. Alongside shame, fear also began to take root. I was terrified at the thought of being exposed for what I had done. What initially seemed like a minor deviation, just a slight detour from my path, soon became a breeding ground for a web of lies that I began to believe. Secondly, my sense of purpose, which had once been crystal clear, disappeared. When I looked in the mirror, I no longer recognized the girl I once was. I felt like a fraud, and I didn't know how to reclaim the person I used to be. I could no longer be her. That version of myself had vanished, leading me to question everything I had once believed about who I was. I lost my identity and felt like a counterfeit.

So rather than allowing my mistake to get me back on course, I surrendered control completely to my mistakes. I convinced myself that this was now my predetermined future. I believed I had to endure the consequences silently until the bitter end. Regrettably, I felt compelled to make amends for my failures and redeem my past mistakes by remaining aboard the sinking ship. I couldn't bring myself to abandon this relationship, as I had invested too much.

The journey that began with me succumbing to a few little lies had a profound impact on my future. Instead of acknowledging my mistakes and placing my trust in the vastness of God's ability to handle them, I allowed myself to be consumed by a cycle of more lies. I believed that by living in shame, I was actively addressing my problem. Holding onto shame became my way of assuming respon-

My heart received the information, that information was stored, and new actions began to pump out of that experience. The heart holds it all.

sibility and seeking penance for the overwhelming guilt I carried. Though it may not have been a productive approach, it provided me with a semblance of taking action and acknowledging the situation.

Holding onto shame became my way of assuming responsibility and seeking penance for the overwhelming guilt I carried.

In our lives, there is no neutral voice that guides us. We are either influenced by the culture around us or by God's wisdom. Absolutely every decision, regardless of its magnitude, is shaped by either a heart that seeks to align with God's will or a heart that prioritizes our own desires.

There is good news, the Bible doesn't have all bad things to say about the heart! In Psalms 37:4 it says, "Take delight in the Lord, and he will give you the desires of your heart." as you keep reading it says, "**commit** your ways to the Lord, **trust** in him and he will act"

You see, since God created us- we are His masterpiece, only He knows what is best for us! He knows our heart's desires!

"No eye has seen, no ear has heard, and no eye has imagined what God has prepared for those who love Him. Both on heaven and on earth."

1 CORINTHIANS 2:9

While we are bombarded with lies from the great deceiver and the world, God remains diligently working behind the scenes on our behalf, patiently waiting for us to seek His guidance. All we need to do is commit ourselves to His ways and place our trust in Him. It is difficult for our finite minds to grasp the vastness of what God has in store for us if only we trust Him. How many failures and hurts must we endure before we recognize that our hearts often lead us astray?

Psalm 37:7 says "Be **still** before the Lord and **wait** patiently for him". Friends, it is a reminder that Jesus, in His kindness, understands our need for clear, practical instructions to guide us in doing what is right. He calls us to commit ourselves to Him, place our trust in Him, find stillness, and patiently wait for His timing. However, He is aware of our struggle to follow these instructions. We often experience moments of wavering faith, doubt, impatience, and a desire to assert our own will. Yet, Jesus not only desires to liberate us from the pain caused by destructive choices and heartbreak, but He also has even greater blessings in store for us. We were intentionally formed with a specific purpose in mind.

Did you know that you are a unique design created by God to walk this earth at this precise moment, destined to fulfill a purpose He has assigned to you? Understanding that we are masterpieces crafted by an artist with a specific goal not only fills us with hope but also grants us a sense of destiny. It is no surprise, then, that the enemy tirelessly seeks to hinder us. Every day, he works overtime to obstruct our connection to God's voice and prevent us from living in the fullness of His Truth. This is precisely why it is crucial for us to immerse ourselves in God's Word. Amidst the multitude of voices that surround us, including those from television, work, friends, and family, God's Word remains the only source of absolute Truth. **It stands as an unwavering and infallible guide for us to navigate through life.**

"Do not conform any longer to the patterns of this world, but be transformed by the renewing of your mind. Then you will be able to test and approve what God's will is, his good pleasing and perfect will".

ROMANS 12:2

When our minds are renewed by the power of God's truth in the Bible, our hearts can better discern the schemes of the enemy.

Though I understand these Truths today, it took me a long time to get here. The web I wove between my heart and mind from that one mistake made me feel trapped, unable to find my way out. So despite my love for God and my desire to follow His will, I was unprepared for the intense battle raging within my heart. Even as God patiently awaited the opportune time to move mountains in my life, I continued to succumb to the lies.

REFLECTION QUESTION

Understanding that the heart is the center of our emotions also helps us understand the areas that we struggle , in what areas have you allowed your heart to deviate just a small click off course?

CHAPTER FOUR

Spiritual Handshakes

Tortured fear and stupid confidence are both desirable states of mind.
- Screwtape Letters

One day, I shook hands with the devil.

Have you ever thought about that? The act of reaching out your hand to take another's... what exactly does it mean? The thing about a handshake is that everyone understands it. Whether you're from China or America, it's a way to greet an acquaintance or a friend, and it's the universal gesture that signifies an agreement, as if to say, "we have a deal."

The spirits of this world are not only real; they hold considerable influence over our lives. Every day, we encounter opportunities to align ourselves with these spirits. In 1 Corinthians, the apostle Paul addressed this issue when he said, "What we have received is not the spirit of the world, but the Spirit who is from God, so that we may understand what God has freely given us." Paul was speaking specifically to those who have dedicated their lives to Christ, highlighting the contrast between the spirit of the world and the Spirit of God. The tactic of these worldly spirits is to whisper into our thoughts and appeal to our desires. Once we allow ourselves to entertain their ideas and draw closer to them, they can easily lead us astray. A mere thought can quickly transform into action. It may seem dramatic, but why do those of us who love Jesus and desire to follow His will continue to engage in behaviors we know we shouldn't? We become frustrated with ourselves, striving each day to improve, only to find ourselves repeating the very actions we despise. Temptations have a way of finding us, even when we don't actively seek them out. And this is no accident.

The Apostle Paul expressed his own struggles in Romans: "I do not understand what I do. For what I want to do I do not do, but what I hate I do." He went on to describe the constant battle in his mind, with evil always present and waging war, despite his genuine delight in God's law. This was a man who deeply loved Jesus and made significant contributions to the New Testament. Yet even he struggled with the allure of the enemy.

I've made some significant agreements with spirits that had no place in my life as a follower of Jesus. However, by accepting and living with my shame while persisting in disobedience, I inadvertently widened the door, allowing more of these spirits to linger. It was like a spiritual handshake, sealing the connection. And my senior year of high school was the epitome of this very principle.

By accepting and living with my shame while persisting in disobedience, I inadvertently widened the door, allowing more of these spirits to linger.

At first glance, my life seemed great. I enjoyed a close bond with my youth pastor and his wife, who genuinely cared for me and imparted truths that continue to shape my life today. They were the ones who recognized my potential and brought out the best in me. Moreover, I cherished the fellowship of my church community and found immense joy in serving God. Whether it was singing on stage, leading small groups, or welcoming newcomers to church, these activities defined my sense of fulfillment and contentment. It was in these moments that I found my true happiness.

"At church, I am important. I am needed" (spiritual handshakes)

But hold on! Why is that considered a spiritual handshake? Aren't those positive things? Indeed, having a strong relationship with my church leaders and feeling valued and needed are good things. However, you will soon discover that Satan has a way of taking something that appears harmless or even beneficial and distorting it. Stick with me here.

Now, when it came to school, it was an entirely different story. Life there proved to be challenging for me. I had sacrificed most of my friendships in exchange for my boyfriend. Throughout the school day, I found myself in survival mode, feeling shut out by my peers at best and resented at worst. I no longer cared or made an effort with these classmates. I convinced myself, "Just one more year, and then I'll be gone." On the surface, I put on a cheerful facade, but deep down, I despised being the outcast, the one who was pushed aside.

"At school, nobody likes me, I'm alone." (spiritual handshakes)

As the weeks turned into months and our relationship persisted, a pattern emerged. More lies, more sins, and more excuses became the norm, and yet I had somehow made peace with them. We found ourselves trapped in a relentless cycle of messing up, seeking for-giveness, promising not to repeat our mistakes, and then falling back into the same patterns. Each time, we would apologize and convince ourselves that this time would be the last. I would remind my boyfriend that we couldn't continue down this path, and he would agree, but we would inevitably allow the tension to simmer until it boiled over once again. Day after day, with each new mistake, I would convince myself that this was the only way. The cycle repeated itself relentlessly. I frequently reminded myself that I was at fault for giving so much of myself away, and now I felt bound to stay in this situation. Of course, I also desired to be with him. He was the only one who truly knew me. I had invested so much of myself in this relationship that I couldn't bear the thought of letting it go. I was deeply committed.

"I'm a failure. Now he's all I have. Don't screw this up too." (spiritual handshakes)

Then it happened, something felt sick within me. Each morning, as I got ready for school, I would sit down, hoping I wouldn't vomit. I couldn't understand what was happening. I attributed my sickness to the stress of feeling isolated at school. However, I also noticed an insistent hunger and a steady weight gain. It was during this time that I realized I couldn't recall the last time I had my period. Pregnant? No. No, no no! It couldn't be true. This simply could not be happening to me. But as denial faded, I found myself making more compromises, engaging in further handshakes leading to harmful actions:

"What will the church think?"

"What will the kids at school think?"

"You will let everyone down!"

"Your mom will know she was right all along!"

"You are so stupid."

"Your life will be OVER!"

^ (All spiritual handshakes)

This is when I reached out my hand for the handshake that changed everything.

It felt as though there was only one way to escape this impossible situation. I saw no other alternative before me. The numerous agreements I had made with these spirits had cast a dark shadow over my life. I found myself in an abyss so black that I couldn't discern a way out. There was nobody with me in this tunnel; I felt totally alone. As I gazed through the tunnel, towards the distant end, I could only see a single option looming before me.

End it. This must be erased. (spiritual handshakes)

The accumulation of my mistakes, mixed with the lies I believed along the way, combined with the handshakes that drew me closer to darkness, has led to this pivotal moment. The blinders were tightly fixed upon my eyes, and we were moving in only one direction: the termination of these mistakes.

Abortion is the only way out of this mess. (spiritual handshakes)

We skipped school and drove the three-hours to the clinic. As I sat in the chair, the doctor attempted to make conversation, but I snapped at her, "I believe this is murder, but I'm trapped with no other choice." Her body language grew visibly uncomfortable, and her eyes reflected unease from my harsh words. However, she swiftly accepted my payment and proceeded with her duties as usual. Tears streamed down my face, and an overwhelming sense of shame engulfed my heart as I ended the life of my child that day.

The following weeks were even darker and more confusing. The emptiness, disappointment, and shame were unbearable. Who had I become? What had I done? While the world around me kept spinning as if nothing had changed- something within me changed. My web of lies isolated me, leaving me on an island with no help in sight. As I tried to draw closer to my boyfriend, he appeared to be pushing me away. **Anger.** Anger at myself, anger at my sin, and anger at my boyfriend for not standing up and questioning our decision. **Fear.** Now what? The solution to our problem didn't solve the problem; it only created more problems. What do I do now? **Stupidity.** What is wrong with me? How could I be so foolish? How could I do such a terrible thing?

The enemy's playbook is small; it always follows the same pattern. He whispers in our ears, coaxing us into making agreements with him. Then, once we've sufficiently shook on it, he heaves on the weight of shame, guilt, and disappointment.

By this point, I should have recognized the havoc caused by these deceitful alliances! And to some extent, I did. However, I couldn't bear the thought of disappointing my friends, family, and church. Instead of releasing my grip on the enemy's hand once and for all, I held on tighter, desperately clinging as if my life depended on it. Not only did I persist in believing the lie of exposure, but after this, it grew stronger and more petrifying.

Remember that initial handshake that appeared harmless? The whisper that reminded me of my significance and how much I was valued at church? I permitted something positive in my life to be exploited for my own imprisonment. I allowed a pedestal to be erected beneath me, and the mere thought of being toppled from it was unbearable. Was I the only Christian who had succumbed to this? Was I the lone churchgoer who had made such a grave mistake? I felt like a fraud, and so another handshake was forged:

"No other real Christian would do the terrible things you've done. Nobody can find out!" (spiritual handshakes)

I finished high school and headed to college, striving to move forward in the best way possible, all the while concealing most of my pain. Gradually, but privately, I began to find healing through God's compassionate love and the gentle whispers of truth that graced my ears. However, this transformation didn't occur effortlessly. It required significant effort on my part. I had to invest emotional and physical energy into excavating the lies. This consumed my time and required daily surrendering of my selfish desires. It also required me to submit all of my thoughts and failures to God. I had to develop the ability to discern the presence of Truth, embodied by God's Holy Spirit. This Spirit gives genuine wisdom to believers and allows them to grasp the "secret and hidden wisdom of God (1 Corinthians 2:7).

God is always waiting to heal our broken-ness and teach us Truth, but we must first take His hand and trust His ways, not our own.

God's loving handshake comes in for the hug!

It turns out that Christ-followers, just like any other individuals in this world, are striving to do our best in combating the voices vying for our attention. As Paul stated, evil constantly lurks, waging war against our minds. Each new day presents us with the choice to extend our hand for the agreements that we have no business making. Every person around us harbors their own set of lies they have embraced and handshakes they have made. No one is immune to the danger of being pulled overboard.

Which is why it's so important to stay away from the edge.

Do we ever completely overcome spiritual handshakes and con-fusion caused by lies? Probably not on this side of Heaven. However, what I do know is that the closer we draw to Jesus, the clearer our perception of Truth becomes. It becomes increasingly difficult for the enemy to deceive us when we intimately know our Father. This transformation doesn't happen without dedicated effort to knowing Jesus, the creator of our souls. **We must actively walk towards Him if we desire to discern the lies.** That is the only way. Through this process, I have learned to recognize the enemy's voice, see through his tricks, and established my true belonging.

My gratitude is great!

The handshakes do not make Satan the winner. In fact, the handshakes are the very reasons why Jesus came! His love for me (and you!) is so profound that He foresaw my stumbling and falling. Jesus loves us so much that He takes our worst parts and utilizes them to facilitate our growth and transformation. He took my failures and employed them to grant me freedom. Through them, He nurtured my wisdom and maturity. Jesus articulated this beautifully in Luke when He said, "She was forgiven many, many sins, and so she is very grateful. If the forgiveness is minimal, the gratitude is minimal." Luke 7:47

I am amazed each day by the love and kindness that Jesus has shown. I know that nobody can love me as well as He does. His love sees my failures without condemnation and views them as opportunities to produce fruit in my life if I surrender them to Him and bring them into the light.

Thank you, Jesus, for loving us so well. You take our failures and make them our **freedom**! All we need to do is lay them at Your feet. We have the authority to look them straight in the eye and say, 'I will not believe another lie. I am not going to make an agreement today with anyone or anything other than my Creator.' How do we do that? First we must establish what is Truth. What does my Creator say about me?

He says I am fearfully and wonderfully made! (truth)

I am a masterpiece! (truth)

My sins are as far as the East is from the West! (truth)

I am forgiven. I am loved. I am redeemed!! (truth)

It's time we learn the ways of the spirits of this world and how to be spiritually awake. We have more control over the spiritual realm than we think. We just need to be attentive and discern, listening for lies. It starts with knowing our father and being in close proximity to Him.

A WORD TO THOSE WHO'VE ALSO WALKED THIS ROAD.

As years have gone by and I have shared my story with more people, I've found that there are many others who have also ended their pregnancies—some Christian girls, others not. Some feel deep remorse, others not as much. The way my story played out and the feelings I experienced may not mirror yours. You may not have felt guilt or shame for going through with it; perhaps you felt relief. Alternatively, your confusion and remorse may have set in long after your termination. I pray that my story does not compound shame or guilt onto yours. Maybe you still aren't sure if it was the wrong choice for you. Whatever you may be feeling, know that wrestling with our decisions is healthy. Contemplating is good. However, when shame creeps in, don't take the bait! Don't shake the hand of the enemy. Shame does not bring healing; it only brings more condemnation, which leads to more poor choices. I pray that the Truth of God's love will dispel these lies. You are loved, and you are not defined by your mistakes.

God redeems all things; we only
need to give Him our hand!

Spiritual Handshakes: If you can reflect on your own thoughts and desires, what handshakes have you made in the past and are currently making today? Keeping in mind, any negative thoughts about yourself, do not reflect who God says you are. What thoughts need to be expelled to bring you closer to who God made you to be?

How can God use your failures for good? If you cannot think of any good that could come from your mistakes, I challenge you to talk with a trusted mentor about them. You will find so much healing through communication and community. Let others speak life into your mistakes!

Have you fully surrendered your life to God? If the answer is no, what is holding you back?

CHAPTER FIVE:

The Mustard Seed Dies

"For truly I tell you, if you have faith the size of a mustard seed, you will say to this mountain, 'Move from here to there,' and it will move; and nothing will be impossible for you."
-Matthew 17:20-21

I joined the Army National Guard and headed off to basic training before my second year of college. Unfortunately, this was also the time when my mother's health began to deteriorate. The years of pill bottles lining our counter took its toll. While I endured the mental and physical challenges imposed by my drill sergeants, my mother was battling the merciless demon known as cancer. But I firmly believed that the Lord would grant her healing. With unwavering conviction, I eagerly anticipated the day my mother would become a living testament to God's healing power. Prayer became a constant in my life as I sought divine intervention. I genuinely believed that God was guiding me in this direction, and I anxiously waited for the moment when His plans would unfold. The motto that sustained me throughout this difficult time was the "faith of a mustard seed." Clinging to this motto and clutching her hand, I patiently waited for the Lord to work out His miracle.

She was in and out of the hospital quite a few times that summer, but we only viewed those stays as minor setbacks, never fully considering the severity of her failing health. This was despite the presence of bruising all over her body, extreme fatigue, and the gray undertones of her skin. She was my mom, and when it comes to those we love, their appearance doesn't matter. It's like God protects us, placing a filter over our eyes and enabling us to only see them as they are- people we love. Family. Some might call it denial, but I think of it the way a parent sees their child. Even if they are a mess, we perceive our kids as the most beautiful and wonderful creations on earth. Their messy mouths are adorable, and their stinky feet are just too cute. We have no problem wiping their snotty noses or cleaning their dirty bums. Our love runs so deep that we see beauty, just like Jesus sees us. We may be a mess, constantly failing, and constantly in need of forgiveness, but Jesus sees His child. He responds by extending His hand and pulling us up. He sees the mess in our lives and reaches out to us anyway. He says, 'I love you' as He wipes our tears. He responds, 'You are forgiven' as He cleans up the messes we've made.

> *We may be a mess, constantly failing, and constantly in need of forgiveness, but Jesus sees His child.*

For the Fourth of July, we purchased fireworks and set up lawn chairs on an empty field outside of town. On that particular day, my mom felt great. The medication was doing its job, and she had more energy than I had seen in a long time. I was thrilled to see her spunky and full of life, even if it was just for a few hours. After all the fireworks had been set off and we were driving back home, she insisted that my dad stop at a fireworks stand. None of us understood why she wanted to make another purchase. She emerged from the tent with bags and bags of poppers, the kind where you pull the string from the plastic champagne bottle and colorful streamers shoot out.

"What in the world are you buying all those things for?" I asked, bewildered. She responded with utmost confidence, "They're for your wedding!" With that, she settled herself in the car and gave dad the green light to head home.

My wedding?! It made no sense to me. There were no wedding plans in my foreseeable future. Yet, there she was, going into a fireworks stand in the middle of the night to purchase all their poppers for my supposed wedding. We all speculated that she must have been overtired or that the medication might have been working too well! Nevertheless, we returned home, grateful that Mom had such a good day. It was a joyful Independence Day, truly embodying the spirit of freedom. After being bound by pain and fatigue for so long, witnessing my mom come alive, laughing, and freely moving around, even with the help of medication, was a beautiful sight.

Unfortunately, our taste of freedom didn't last long. The following month, we found ourselves back in the hospital with her. After spending a weekend at the Mayo Clinic by her side, the doctors advised us to go home and return after the work week. My siblings and I made the exhausting five-hour drive back home, while my dad stayed at the hospital with her. There didn't seem to be any immediate cause for concern, and we held onto our belief, "Faith of a mustard seed." I had no doubt that she would recover and be out of the hospital shortly, as had happened so many times before. Late that night, we arrived home, utterly drained from the emotional stress of having a loved one in the hospital. I collapsed onto the bed and quickly drifted off to sleep.

The next morning disoriented and still groggy from a short night's sleep, I was abruptly awakened by the piercing sound of my sister's screams and cries, urging me to get out of bed. I struggled to gather my thoughts and comprehend her words. "We need to go back! She's dying! We have to hurry!" She dashed around the house in a state of panic. Dying? What was she saying? It didn't make sense to me. The doctor had assured us that everything would be fine until the weekend!? She wasn't sick enough to die. She still had so much life ahead of her! I needed her! WE ALL needed her! I held tightly onto my faith, firmly believing that God would heal her. I couldn't let go of that "faith of a mustard seed' promise.

We got in the car and drove the five-hours back to the hospital. As I settled into the backseat, I immersed myself in reading my Bible and praying fervently. My attention was drawn to Matthew 17:20, which says, 'If you have the faith of a mustard seed, you can move mountains.' With unwavering faith, I trusted that today, God would provide His miracle. Today we would witness the divine intervention in my mother's life.

We entered her hospital room, and the sight was worse than I had anticipated. A ventilator was inserted in her mouth, rendering her unable to speak. Her eyes remained open, and tears of jaundice streamed down her cheeks, each yellow droplet falling onto her pillow. It struck me how I had never seen tears that color before. Despite her inability to communicate verbally, she locked eyes with my brother, her gaze filled with unspoken words. It was agonizing to witness my mom's struggle to express herself with the ventilator obstructing her speech.

Although I felt apprehensive about praying for healing in front of all the people gathered around her bed, I mustered the courage and prayed boldly. "Lord, you have said that even faith as small as a mustard seed can move mountains. I beg you, God, to move this mountain and heal my mom!" And as the words left my mouth, life left my mother's body. Just like that, she closed her eyes and disappeared. Of course a body still lay in front of us, but my mom wasn't in it. She had left the room.

How can this be? How could my prayer be met with death? I trusted His promise! When my mom died, my mustard seed dream died right beside her. And in that moment, something else within me also died: my faith.

I could never have imagined that the day before would be the last time I heard my mom's voice. I never thought that just 24 hours ago would mark my final opportunity to seek her guidance or ask her questions. I stood there, consumed by confusion, while everyone around me wept. This was not how it was supposed to happen! And now, I am left without a mom. She's gone. And I wasted the last three years of our time together in pointless battles: fighting for control, fighting for my own desires, and fighting over a boy. Arguments and time squandered. Now, she is gone, and I am left with neither.

So many losses surfaced in the aftermath of my mom's death. I lost my virginity, my baby, my boyfriend, my unanswered prayers, and the ultimate blow... my mom. It shattered my ability to trust in so many things. There was no joy, only an overwhelming sense of loss. I no longer felt God's love and protection. I felt forgotten. My trust and belief in the book that had governed my life were shattered. Everything I had been taught growing up seemed feeble and irrelevant in the face of my pain and frustration. Confusion consumed me, and anger surged within. My faith in God dissolved. Where was my miracle? I certainly didn't feel loved or seen as the Bible suggests. My joy vanished, and hope along with it. I lost hope in the prospect of good things to come. Trusting in hope felt too risky. It felt too risky to hope for a brighter tomorrow or for joy to emerge from sorrow, or even to trust that people or God wouldn't let me down. I concluded that if this was the God I believed in, I had no interest in placing my trust in Him. I doubted His goodness, kindness, and, above all, His Word. I had reached my limit, and with that, I closed my Bible and walked away.

The days following my decision to walk away were... (dare I say) liberating. I felt free, unchained, and unbound from the rules that had dictated my life since birth. Instead of adhering to the expectations imposed by the church, I could now live according to my own rules and personal boundaries. There was no more guilt, no more worries about measuring up or fear of being labeled as "bad." I was released from the confines of religious boundaries. And it felt empowering. I could rely on my own judgment. This way, I no longer had to live in constant fear of losing everything I held dear. I could establish my own boundaries and protect myself from potential pain. I held the control!

As the days turned into months, living according to my own rules was exhilarating. I had no one to answer to, I was unbound and free to live for myself. Gone were the days of overthinking every promise and feeling let down by unfulfilled expectations. For the most part, I remained a good person with a clear moral compass. But the true freedom came from within my own mind. I no longer worried about what others had to say about my life or living up to their expectations. I dismantled all the Christian ideas I had once built. I began questioning everything I had held as truth. What did I truly know about Jesus? Was he both a man and God? Could I trust the Bible, the book that had let me down, as Truth? These questions troubled my heart. I felt betrayed by all my previous beliefs. My perspective on others shifted as well, and I discovered a whole new world filled with extraordinary people. Many of them didn't follow God, yet their hearts were as kind as any saint I could imagine. I realized that much of my theology had been shaped by human interpretations and the teachings of the church, rather than a direct connection with Jesus and His teachings. I enjoyed this life free from the pressure to live up to the expectations of others.

Faith of a mustard seed. That loss was the breaking point for this downward spiral. The lies I believed leading up to my mom's death contributed to my lack of faith. But losing my mom shattered my trust. How could a loving father take my mother away? I was too young, and we all needed her so much! Despite the immense pain, this blow became a stepping stone in my personal faith journey. At that time, I couldn't see it, but there was still a glimmer of faith hiding deep within me.

God knows us better than we know ourselves, and He uses every failure and setback to help us grow into our best selves. While I was in the process of discovering my true identity, God had to guide me in releasing the burden of living up to others' expectations. It was like a mountain that needed to be moved within my own life. And to be honest, I'm still moving that mountain, daily.

This "Faith of a mustard seed..." verse still challenges me. I comprehend the concept of faith, but the idea of moving mountains is perplexing. I'm unsure if we can fully grasp the profound meaning God intended behind it. However, one valuable lesson I have learned is that the emphasis lies in the size of our faith rather than the size of the mountain. God only asks for a small amount, like a mustard seed. This tiny seed, when nurtured, can produce a towering tree.

*It only takes the tiniest bit of faith, and
God has the power to help it flourish!*

He understands our questions and is capable of handling our doubts. He only asks for a little faith from us. With even a small amount, He can use it to bring about great things! Deep within me, He was nurturing the soil to help that tiny seed grow. Unaware of

God's constant presence in my life, He was uprooting the weeds of my past foundations and moving me to a place where I could develop strong roots and stand on solid ground. I believed I was in control, but God utilizes everything for His purpose. I thought God was the source of my problems, but He was actually working behind the scenes to bring about solutions. My resentment didn't deter Him from continuing the good work He initiated in me years ago. He is so limitless that He can handle our anger towards Him. Some of us may take the long way around, but God is big enough to handle that as well.

"And I am sure of this, that He who began a good work in you will bring it to completion at the day of Jesus Christ."

PHILIPPIANS 1:6

When are the times in your life that you have felt "let down" by God? How have those instances shaped who you believe God is?

When reflecting honestly, are you trusting in God's plans or are you expecting God to fulfill your own? Even when our desires are honorable, God may have different plans. How submitted are you to God, IF His plans are not yours?

CHAPTER SIX:

Spiritually Awake

"It is not objective proof of God's existence that we want but the experience of God's presence. That is the miracle we are really after…"
-Brennan Manning, The Ragamuffin Gospel

Years later, I still vividly recall the anger and confusion I felt in the days following my mother's death. I remember the feeling of frustration as I questioned why a loving God would take her so soon. I was desperate for her presence, and I believed her presence in our lives was needed. Her life was cut short, a mere 50 years, and mine had barely begun.

I have spent my entire adulthood navigating life without her guiding hand. I have now lived longer without her on this earth, than with her. Yet, as the hands of time continue their march, I have discovered a surprising truth—a fact I hate to admit- I didn't actually need her as desperately as I had once believed. In fact, I have not only survived but dare I say, I have even thrived. We all have. It is a somber reality that we are often mistaken about the true necessities of life. Certainly, we desired our mother's love and support. We longed for her guidance and companionship. I'd probably be a better cook, if she were here. However, the distinction between wants and needs is frequently blurred. We arrogantly assume we know what is best for ourselves, presuming to play God by dictating what He should do to make our lives complete. We meticulously plan our futures and set goals to fulfill our personal desires. Yet, if we are truly honest with ourselves, it is not inherent in our nature to desire what God deems best. How often do we consult Him first? We devote ourselves to preserving a life of happiness and freedom from pain, and rightfully so, for nobody seeks affliction, struggles, or death. However, the harsh reality is that each of us will encounter affliction, face struggles, and eventually confront death. They are the reality of our fallen story. But let us not misinterpret these adversities as reflections of God's character. God is still good! The Bible encourages us...

*"Who shall separate us from the love of Christ? Shall **trouble** or **hardship** or **persecution** or **famine** or **nakedness** or **danger** or **sword**? As it is written: "For your sake we face death all day long; We are considered as sheep to be slaughtered. No, in all these things we are more than conquerors through him who loved us. For I am convinced that neither death nor life, neither angels nor demons, neither the present nor the future, nor any powers, neither height nor depth, nor anything else in all creation, will be able to separate us from the love of God that is in Christ Jesus our Lord."*

ROMANS 8:35-39 NIV

We should anticipate hardships and struggles in life. The Bible serves as a reminder of this harsh reality, urging us to be prepared. However, we often forget this truth and, even more regrettably, become resentful towards God when faced with these situations. Thankfully, we can also anticipate finding peace in Christ during these difficult times. He is by our side, offering comfort to the brokenhearted and rescuing those whose spirits are crushed.

It is precisely in our moments of weakness and greatest pain that Jesus performs His most profound work.

As time marched on, after my mother's passing, the allure of living by my own rules, detached from Christ, gradually faded. There was a persistent sense that God was alive and actively involved in my life. That tiny seed of faith, barely recognizable, had blossomed into a restlessness that yearned for more. I discovered that I could no longer find contentment in living according to my own whims and desires. My mind circled around a pivotal question: What do I truly believe? Where do I stand in my faith? The time had come for me to make a definitive decision. Exhaustion overwhelmed me from harboring anger towards God, and I grew weary of assuming control over my own life. A profound unsettling was within me, gently guiding me back to the embrace of God's Truth.

In the depths of my spirit, I held on tightly to the undeniable Truth that there was more to this life. I knew, without a shadow of a doubt, that we were not alone on this earth. The existence of good and evil was tangible to me. Throughout the years, I experienced both sides in profound ways. As a child, I encountered the chilling embrace of darkness when I gazed into that basement mirror, haunted by voices calling to me. The weight of darkness enveloped me when I gave myself away for the first time, suffocating in a bed of shame. And the depths of darkness engulfed me as I lay on that cold clinic table, where doctors rushed to take life out from within me. Witnessing my mother's deteriorating health and her agonizing battle against illness also exposed me to the grip of darkness.

As real as all that evil was, I also experienced the radiant beauty of God's light. I vividly recall the moment as a young child when I prayed for the Holy Spirit to enter my life. The joy within my heart was so overwhelming that as I ran out of the bible camp chapel, it propelled me to run and leap with uncontainable joy. My little heart raced as swiftly as my feet carried me through the lush summer grass. I never wanted to stop praising Jesus that day as He showered me with His love.

But above all, I found myself reflecting on a pivotal moment that occurred just three years prior, where evil and good collided within me. I was devastated by the break-up with my boyfriend. The result of all our mistakes together sent us in different directions rather than bringing us together. We harbored resentment towards one another, burdened by the pain we both endured during that fateful day at the abortion clinic. As I lay on the couch in my family room, sinking deeper into despair, my emotions consumed me, and a profound sense of failure overwhelmed me. I felt utterly alone, accompanied only by the haunting shadow of guilt. I had lost my boyfriend, most of my friends, and damaged my relationship with my mother. Feeling as though I was suffocating, I stared up at the ceiling, overwhelmed beyond measure. Sinking. My tears refused to flow, and each breath became a struggle. Sinking Deeper.

I was empty, I felt totally alone, and the world looked black.

In that very moment, the darkest of my life, something extraordinary happened. As I looked up toward the ceiling, I felt a divine spirit enter the room. It descended from above, tangible yet invisible to my eyes. Its presence enveloped me like the warmth of a perfect summer day. Suddenly, I felt the burden of sorrow and pain lift off of me. I inhaled heavenly peace as tears streamed down my face. Words struggled to escape my lips, as I was caught in awe. I strained my eyes, desperate to see the "something" that was obviously present. I willed my eyes to open wider, yearning for a glimpse, but as I gazed up at the ceiling, a brilliant light bypassed my eyes and permeated my soul. Pure peace washed over me, and in that moment, nothing else in the world mattered. The Holy Spirit met me in the depths of my darkness. No spoken words were exchanged, yet my soul heard everything. "You are loved. You are forgiven. You are mine." These profound truths resonated within me, spoken directly to my broken heart. It was this moment of beauty and perfection that forever altered the course of my life. Like a gentle embrace, a warm and comforting presence wrapped around me, providing the love and peace I desperately needed at that exact moment. Although this holy encounter was momentary, it became the very catalyst that saved my life.

The Holy Spirit met me in the depths of my darkness.

Darkness and Light, Evil and Good - I knew they both existed. I couldn't deny the reality of the spiritual world. As I reflected on my life and my encounters with light and darkness, I knew I had to make a definitive decision. I couldn't remain angry at God forever. I was tired of running, and I was tired of pushing Him away.

Anger is exhausting. It not only consumes energy but also drains your best energy.

I didn't agree with God's choice to allow cancer to take my mom away, but I also knew that God didn't approve of the choice I made with my child. We tend to blame God for what He does or doesn't do in our lives, but how often do we consider the ways in which we've hurt Him? How often do we consider our own selfishness? I have made many terrible choices despite knowing the better alternatives. I have needlessly made life much harder for myself, even while holding a roadmap that guides me towards a smoother path.

I saw the choices clearly before me, and I realized that my only option was to forgive God and release my anger. It was the only choice that made sense. With that realization, I made a decision: "Okay, God, I acknowledge your existence. I may not understand Your ways, but I surrender control. I am starting over. I am releasing my anger and placing my trust in Your plan. I will let go and have faith that Your ways are better." I stepped back into faith, while having numerous questions and reservations. My journey with Jesus began again, and I took my first step towards discovering who He truly was, understanding my own identity, and determining the path to follow from there.

This transformation didn't occur overnight. The good news is that God is incredibly patient with us. Trust was gradually built as I immersed myself in Scripture and made a conscious effort to make better choices. I didn't pretend to have everything figured out, but I established some fundamental boundaries in my relationships. I resolved to stop getting hurt. I made a firm decision that I would guard my heart and not give it away until I found my future husband. And this time, I meant it.

It is indeed crucial for us to become aware of the spiritual realm and its influence in our lives. Do you have an unsettling, a yearning for more? Maybe you can't quite put your finger on it, but it could be Jesus calling you to Him! Rest assured, even if we may not perceive it, we are being pursued.

"Be alert and of sober mind. Your enemy the devil prowls around like a roaring lion waiting for someone to devour."

1 PETER 5:8

The spirits of this world want to treat us like marionettes- puppets on a string- manipulating our decisions and changing our script. We have been equipped by God to unveil the mysteries between our physical world and the spiritual realm, enabling us to perceive things as they truly are. God has granted us the necessary tools to cut the ties that hold us to the enemy. We can discern between good and evil, distinguish light from darkness, and gain confidence to live the purpose we were meant to live.

REFLECTION QUESTIONS:

Throughout scripture Jesus was close to the broken-hearted. He rescued those whose spirits were crushed and he wants to do the same for you! Can you recall times in your life when Jesus comforted you? Write these moments down in the front of your heart! This is the God who loves us and knows us better than we know ourselves! Reflect on and thank Him for His kindness.

The closer we draw to Jesus, the more we scare the enemy. It is the Christ follower whom the enemy tries to devour! Ask God to show you the areas where you may be being manipulated by the enemy. God wants to help you see Truth, but you first need to be honest about the areas you've allowed the enemy to influence. Prayerfully considering, What are those areas that first come to mind?

CHAPTER SEVEN:

Puppets on a String

"You will be accepted if you do what is right. But if you refuse to do what is right, then watch out. Sin is crouching at the door, eager to control you. But you must subdue it and be its master."
-Genesis 4:7

PART 1

Not everything is as it seems around here, **the spirits of this world will play you like a puppet if you let them.** These spirits coexist with our earthly realm, living alongside us, whispering into our ears, and seeking to exert control over our thoughts and choices. If we fail to acknowledge this, they will manipulate us like marionettes in the grand performance known as 'Life.' However, there is hope. We have the capacity to discern the script more clearly. The veil that separates our world from the spiritual realm is gradually thinning, and it can be lifted, enabling us to distinguish between truth and deception.

Allow me to introduce you to the cast of characters in this production. First and foremost, we have God, the original playwright and creator of this world and everything within it. However, there are a few members of His ensemble who have chosen to rebel and attempt to seize control. These individuals are well-versed in the script but disagree with its intended conclusion. Their aim is to alter the story and bring us down with them. Running the show of this renegade crew is a figure you may be familiar with but prefer to disregard: Satan. Although he may not always be directly involved, he employs numerous stagehands to carry out his agenda. These assistants are skilled at subtly diverting our paths off course. To recognize their influence when they speak to us, we must be attuned to their tactics. Once we learn how to discern their words, we can protect our hearts and stay on guard. Regrettably, I must admit that I have not always been vigilant. There have been moments when I allowed my mind and heart to wander, thereby exposing myself to the enemy's script. Here are a few of the deceptive messages they have whispered to me, and likely, to you as well.

DOUBT. SHAME. FEAR. PARTIAL TRUTHS (AKA LIES).

Doubt. I am prone to doubt. Some of us are naturally more skeptical, needing to unravel things on our own. This quality can be beneficial if channeled appropriately, but it can also be exploited against us. In my younger years, doubt became one of the first strings that connected me to the enemy's influence. Initially, I doubted my mother, questioning whether she understood my experiences and emotions. Then, I began doubting the significance of the missteps I took in the wrong direction. I convinced myself that it wasn't that serious, that crossing the line just slightly wouldn't cause much harm. Next, I doubted God's wisdom when He took my mother from me. I questioned His goodness and doubted the truthfulness of His word.

*These doubts progressively distanced me
from the Truth and positioned me squarely
within the confines of the enemy's script.*

Satan employed a similar tactic with Adam and Eve when he enticed Eve to take a bite from the forbidden fruit. He sowed a tiny seed of doubt in her mind, causing her to question the Truth of God's words. We cannot fathom the duration or the multitude of ways in which he approached her, injecting doubts and questioning thoughts into her mind. Nevertheless, over time, she succumbed to his influence and yielded to temptation by reaching for that apple. (After all, did it truly matter if she took just one bite from the tree? It seemed like such a trivial act, and perhaps there was more knowledge that God was withholding from them.) Satan twisted God's words and skillfully ensnared her with his strings. This seed of doubt grew into mankind's first sin.

Even now, doubts continue to infiltrate my mind. I question my worth and doubt my abilities as a parent. In fact, at times, I even doubt whether anyone will read this book! (So, thank you for that!) However, I have grown wiser through experience. With practice, I have developed the ability to identify doubts as they arise and confront them directly. It is crucial to capture these doubtful thoughts when they try to invade our minds. By recognizing them for what they are, we can

*Doubts do not
represent the
Truth; they are
merely questions.*

actively combat their influence. Doubts do not represent the Truth; they are merely questions. When a doubt emerges, it is important to reframe it as such.

Do I have value? Yes. We all do!

Am I a good parent? Yes. I am doing the best I can.

Will anyone read this book? Again, yes. And even if they don't... so what.

Doubts do not come from Truth. Usually, they are based in fear. And this type of fear always lies to us. This is not a healthy fear. It's the kind that tells us, "WORRY! Panic!" And that is not from God.

Doubt=Fear and Fear=Lies

So, when doubt creeps into my mind, I am faced with a choice regarding how to handle that thought. I refuse to identify with it. Instead, I will scrutinize and acknowledge that the thought does not align with the word of God. I will no longer allow doubt to cling to me because I know that doubt never comes from our maker.

"But let him ask in faith, with no doubting, for the one who doubts is like a wave of the sea that is driven and tossed by the wind."

JAMES 1:6

Shame. Shame was a leading lady in my story. Most of my actions as a teenager were guided by shame. Shame is the voices in your head that tell you how _____ you are. Insert any choice word: terrible, ugly, embarrassing, unworthy, fat, stupid....you get the point. And the hardest part? Shame feels true. Just like doubt.

What will people think? (Most likely not what you're creating in your mind)

You will never do better. (Lie.)

You should never tell anyone! (Lie.)

You are _____ . (Lie.)

How many young people and adults internalize this dialogue

and accept it as truth? Unfortunately, the answer is far too many. Moreover, there are individuals who have listened to these voices for so long that they have become part of their identity. They have become accustomed to the constant presence of shame, dictating their every action. Its influence is subtle and persuasive, as Brene Brown aptly describes, "Shame derives its power from being unspeakable." Shame urges you to remain silent, encouraging you to keep your struggles hidden. "Shame thrives on secret keeping." However, the only way to break free from shame's grip is to voice it aloud. It requires exposing it to the light, bringing it out into the open. This entails sharing your experience with someone, quite possibly the very person whom shame is compelling you to keep it from. And, man, that is hard. When such a powerful force is telling you to hide, it takes tremendous bravery to bring it to light. But let me encourage you and share a secret with you that the enemy doesn't want you to know. Are you ready for it? Lean into this: Whatever you think will happen, most likely won't. Shame lies to you. My shame told me, **"Don't tell anyone!** They will judge you! They won't forgive you." And in my life, 100% of the time, the voice of shame has been wrong! Do you hear that? This is important. Shame's goal is to keep you alone in your thoughts! Shame will do whatever it can to make sure you don't tell anyone about your struggles.

> *Shame wants to keep you in*
> *bondage to your failures.*

I imagine there are many others who have found themselves in a similar situation as me, cradling shame like a fragile baby and living with fear as a constant companion. If those words, "Nobody can EVER find out," have become ingrained in your mental vocabulary, it serves as a clear indicator that you are being deceived. When fear, panic, and pain grip your gut at the mere thought of exposure, it signifies that the great deceiver has gained a foothold in your mind and heart. And I assure you; this is a complete lie. Whatever scenarios you have concocted in your mind as a result of potential exposure are most likely unfounded. I have become all too familiar with the voice of shame speaking over me. I have heard that voice resound loudly on numerous occasions. And for years, I heeded its call. It felt so true. However, I distinctly remember the moment when I summoned the courage to share my story with others. It was a culmination of maturity and sheer exhaustion from hiding. In those instances, I decided to challenge the fear of losing people's love or respect. Without fail, their responses were nothing like what I had anticipated. Every single time, they demonstrated compassion and acceptance, not anger and disgust. The shock of their response never ceases to amaze me, and their love and kindness continue to astound me. I am still taken aback by the jarring contrast between how convincing the lies felt until they were brought into the light through honesty. The voice of shame turned out to be a complete fraud.

When we keep our failures hidden, we deprive ourselves of the opportunity to heal and move forward. To experience true healing, it is essential to bring our sins into the light. This is the only way to eliminate them completely. Confession and seeking forgiveness from God are crucial steps in this process. However, there are situations where it is necessary to disclose our actions to another person in order to find healing. I understand that the thought of doing so can be frightening, and it may seem like the lies surrounding the situation will only grow stronger. It may feel impossible, with so much at stake. However, let us recall what was mentioned in chapter one: the best things in life are often the most challenging. If we desire healing, we must confront the darkness within our lives and expose it to the light. Rise to the challenge!

"But everything exposed by the light becomes visible and everything that is illuminated becomes a light."

EPHESIANS 5:13

Darkness remains concealed until it is brought forth into the light. There is profound hope in the realization that when we expose our darkness, it transforms into light. We can find solace in the belief that Jesus works all things together for our ultimate good.

Is that you? Do you keep your struggles hidden because of the fear of exposure? Perhaps you're afraid of the consequences of speaking the truth? I understand how challenging this can be. For years, I sought refuge behind the false sense of security that shame provided me. However, concealed struggles will persist as struggles, and hidden lies will persist as lies. You cannot truly experience freedom while being controlled by the strings of the enemy! The only way for shame to dissipate is through exposure! We must bring it into the light and cut the strings.

There is profound hope in the realization that when we expose our darkness, it transforms into light.

"Everyone who believes in Him will not be put to shame."

ROMANS 10:11

PART 2

Vulnerability and honesty are the only ways out of shame. And courage is what we need to get there.

Having courage can be challenging and overwhelming at times

but taking the first step is often the most difficult. God has instilled courage within each and every one of us, even if we may not always feel it. Courage is like a muscle that can grow and strengthen with practice. The more we exercise courage, the more it will develop within us. Begin with small acts of courage today, and you will witness the transformation of that courage into something greater in your future. Embrace a life lived courageously, and observe the profound changes it can bring. It's a testament to the beauty that can emerge from difficult circumstances.

Fear. Fear IS a liar! It tells you that your doubts and shame are true. It urges you to run and hide. Yet, fear is the opposite of Godliness. Are you being controlled by fear? If fear dominates your life, the remedy is found in drawing closer to God.

"God is perfect love, and perfect love casts out fear."

1 JOHN 4:18

When my children have a scary dream at night, they promptly leave their beds and rush to our room, seeking comfort. It doesn't take long for our soothing words and loving embrace to alleviate their fears. The same holds true for our Heavenly Father. God, as the perfect parent, will soothe all our fears if we approach Him and allow His comforting words to bring healing.

"When I am afraid, I put my trust in You. In God, whose word I praise - in God I trust. I will not be afraid. What can man do to me?"

PSALM 56:3-4

Like courage, we all have fears established within us, but fear is much more apparent. Of course, there is a healthy fear that serves a purpose. It is beneficial for us to experience fear when faced with a tiger ready to pounce on us. This fear response instructs us to flee, and it is a good thing. This type of fear, bestowed upon us by God, ensures our safety and aids our survival. However, this is not the fear I am addressing here. The fear that leads us to ask questions like "What if?" is not working in our favor. This fear creates a future that isn't real and needs to be put under submission! We must aim to control fear so that it no longer controls us. Keep exercising that courage muscle and watch fear shrink.

Building courage is hard but living in doubt, fear and shame is harder!

Pay attention to your internal dialogue. What fears are being used against you? What are the "What if" scenarios holding you back? We all have specific fears that will keep us stuck, if we let them. By understanding ourselves better, we can become more adept at becoming the best versions of ourselves.

And, most importantly, immerse yourself in the Word of God. Read, study, and commit it to memory! Allow God to eradicate all fear within you. Let the powerful message of His Word dispel the falsehoods and reveal what true godly fear entails—the type of fear that works in our favor. Refuse to grant unhealthy fear any power in your life. Cultivate your courage and have faith that you are a child of the true King, the author of everything! Seek solace in Him and let Him provide you comfort. I promise He will if you ask.

"Even though I walk through the valley of the shadow of death, I will fear no evil, for you are with me; your rod and your staff, they comfort me."

PSALM 23:4

Partial Truths. (Lies) Satan's primary tactic is to mimic God. Devoid of original ideas, he cunningly utilizes God's own concepts. Every action he takes is based on a biblical Truth, which he maliciously distorts. Hence, it is crucial to discern the difference.

In the garden, he deceived Eve by claiming that if she consumed the forbidden fruit, her eyes would be opened, and she would be like God. There was some truth to his statement as her eyes were indeed opened, and she did acquire knowledge. However, she swiftly discovered that she was not truly like God, and her life did not improve as a result. Satan manipulated the truth just enough, planting seeds of doubt within Eve until she succumbed to his deceitful trap.

Leaning on God's word is vital to our success at recognizing the lies of the enemy. When we know His Words, we will recognize Satan's lies. If we don't know His Words, the truth within the enemy's lies will sound very enticing!

The spiritual realm has displayed itself numerous times throughout my life. Despite having made many regrettable choices, I am grateful to have absolute certainty that good and evil are present and actively at work. Without these encounters, I can honestly admit that I would not attribute my fears, doubts, and half-truths to Satan and his demons. Instead, like many others, I would consider them as normal aspects of the human experience, failing to recognize them as attacks on God's creation. Doubt, fear, and partial truths serve as the tools employed to drag us down and keep us tethered to the enemy's grip. Break free. I know you can do it! You are not forced to follow that script!

As I reflect on those years in the past when I was entangled in doubt and fear, the weight of my mistakes became overwhelming. I found myself hiding in shame, succumbing to the lies that kept me trapped within my own mind. Unbeknownst to me, I was being held captive by the enemy. However, when the Holy Spirit intervened, He severed the strings that bound me and lifted me out, granting me a freedom I had never experienced before. Moreover, I was enwrapped in a love that words cannot adequately describe. Stepping away from the enemy's stage, I realized that I had been following the wrong script. Once again, I could perceive clearly the truth of my identity and who truly held control. It was a revelation that I belonged to God, and it was He who was ultimately in charge.

But the most beautiful thing about following God? When He cut the strings that the enemy had attached, He didn't tie me to new strings; God set me free! He doesn't want to dictate what we do in life; He wants us to live freely! He doesn't want us to be held down. He loves us so much that He desires freedom to govern our lives. He will always be there to guide and direct us if we ask, but He won't interfere. He won't force His hand.

"Now the Lord is the Spirit, and where the Spirit of the Lord is, there is freedom."

2 CORINTHIANS 3:17

You see, God loves you and me so deeply that He patiently waits until the times when we need Him the most, and then He comes and surpasses our expectations. His intervention appears unexpectedly, without warning, and in ways we could never anticipate. Jesus understands our needs and knows precisely when to fulfill them. It is futile to try to comprehend Him; instead, we must trust that His perfect timing orchestrates everything. His ways are superior to ours.

As you read these pages, my prayer is that the gentle, sweet, and beautiful spirit descends and takes residence in your heart as well. May it sever the strings that are holding you down and fill you with the same peace and warmth that embraced me all those years ago. God sees you. He loves you. And he would love to take your hand and pull you off that stage.

God brings peace.

SATAN BRINGS FEAR.

God brings conviction.

SATAN BRINGS SHAME.

God brings clarity.

SATAN BRINGS CONFUSION.

God brings love.

SATAN BRINGS CONFLICT.

God brings joy.

SATAN BRINGS PAIN.

God is Truth.

SATAN IS LIES.

"It is for freedom that Christ has set us free. Stand firm, then, and do not let yourselves be burdened again by a yoke of slavery."

GALATIANS 5:1

"He redeems your life from the pit and crowns you with love and compassion."

PSALM 103:4

REFLECTION QUESTIONS:

Doubt. Shame. Fear. Partial Truths (aka lies): The first step towards healing is always admitting the hidden areas we struggle.

Can you list some of the areas where doubt is distancing you from Truth?

Shame reminds you of all of the ways you have failed and must keep hidden. Don't believe this lie anymore! This is your time to bravely share those areas with someone you trust. Run, don't walk towards seeing how doing this will bring so much healing in your life! With whom will you share those hidden failures? How did they respond? How do you feel after exposing them to light?

What are the fears you rehearse in your thoughts? It is time to submit them to the authority of God's word! Rehearse what God's word says about it and walk towards freedom!

The only way to combat Satan's lies is by knowing God's word. Make it a priority to read scripture every single day. Even if it's just 5 minutes, commit to learning to listen for those lies. When will you make time each day for quiet time with Jesus and the Bible?

CHAPTER EIGHT:

Prince Charming

"Love is patient, love is kind, it isn't jealous, it doesn't brag, it isn't arrogant, it isn't rude, it doesn't seek its own advantage, it isn't irritable, it doesn't keep a record of complaints, it isn't happy with injustice, but it is happy with the truth. Love puts up with all things, trusts in all things, hopes for all things, endures all things."
-1 Corinthians 13:4-7

I'm a skeptic, as I mentioned in the last chapter. At times, this skepticism has been beneficial, while at other times, it hasn't. It took me years of selfish pursuit and experiencing failures before I realized that my ways were never superior to God's ways. I always had to learn from my own experiences; I couldn't simply rely on someone else's wisdom. However, when I finally surrendered every aspect of my life to God, that's when the magic began to unfold! I embraced the trust that God had a better plan for my life and underwent a complete turnaround. I made the firm decision that I wouldn't give any part of my heart to another person until I was certain they were the one I would marry.

My mom passed away in August, just before my sophomore year of college was about to begin. I was reluctant to return to school; I felt shut down and harbored hidden resentment. However, my sister, who had assumed the role of my mother, insisted that I continue my education. Since I lacked the strength to make decisions for myself, I followed her guidance, although without much enthusiasm or effort. I observed happy people on campus, frustrated by their smiles and laughter. It felt wrong to see the world continue to move on while I was in such pain. Did anyone see me? I felt invisible and alone. I didn't want to move forward. Studying for classes or putting on a smile at work seemed impossible. I longed to immerse myself in my memories and embrace my pain. However, I understood that my mom would have wanted me to persevere.

Dealing with the overwhelming grief of losing my mom was compounded by a period of feeling unnoticed and undesirable by men. When I made my covenant with God, I never anticipated that I would have no prospects! It was confusing why it seemed like nobody showed any interest in me. As a young girl, being seen and admired held significant importance, yet I felt completely invisible. I couldn't even catch a single guy glancing in my direction. It became clear that a significant portion of my validation stemmed from the opposite sex. However, I persevered, prayed, and often found myself shedding tears over my losses and feelings of isolation.

Ultimately, I placed my trust in God. I understood that being alone was preferable to seeking temporary happiness through people or things. I recognized that only God had the power to fill the void within me; nothing else could do so. I mustered the faith that even though I didn't experience the validation and admiration I longed for, God's promises were sufficient. It wasn't an easy path to walk. However, the knowledge that God loved me and that I held inherent worth carried me through this challenging period. By this time, I understood that my feelings often led me astray and that I couldn't rely on them, whether they were present or absent. **I recognized that feelings are not synonymous with truth. So I turned my focus to Truth.**

Reflecting on that season, trusting God was not easy for me. Despite making plans and setting rules for ourselves, our human nature continues to tempt us. Our thoughts persist in telling us lies. The battle between our flesh and our spirit is ongoing, with each vying for control. This dynamic never changes; the only fluctuation lies in which one holds more power. The question is, which one are we feeding, the flesh or the spirit? The one getting fed is the one getting stronger. It is crucial to feed our spirit through prayer, reading the Bible, and engaging with fellow believers in a community. Simultaneously, we must resist the desires of our hearts and counteract the lies propagated by the enemy.

By continuously developing our spiritual strength, we compel the flesh to weaken and lose its hold.

For two years, I held onto what I knew to be true, rather than relying on my fluctuating feelings. Deep within, I knew that God desired good things for my life. I knew that His love for me was unwavering, and His plans for me were the very best. And so, I chose to wait. And wait. And wait. **In our waiting, God always works to produce fruit, even if we fail to recognize it in the moment.** Often, the fruit He brings forth appears different from what we might expect or choose for ourselves. God's fruit doesn't conform to our preconceived notions or imaginations, and yet, this is often how we can know it came from Him.

"My thoughts are nothing like your thoughts," says the Lord. "And my ways are far beyond anything you could imagine."

ISAIAH 55:8

When my Prince Charming finally arrived, it wasn't on a horse. Sadly, my Prince Charming strongly dislikes horses, which I still think somehow God may have fumbled. He wasn't holding a sign of announcement either. I didn't recognize him as my knight since I was too busy looking the other direction! He was a friend from high school. We went to our church youth group together, and I always thought he was attractive (in a 'I want to set you up with my friend' sort of way). He was a farmer, and I was a city girl! He was quiet, and I was the life of the party. We weren't compatible since I was planning to leave town and move to a 'real' city as soon as I graduated from college. I had big plans and dreams for myself, none of which involved my hometown. During college breaks I'd come home and we would hang out together, only as friends, of course. Until the summer, when things shifted. We were spending a lot of time at his lake cabin, and I began to feel a spark. There was a stirring in my heart. Doesn't water and sunsets always seem to do that?! I also started feeling frustrated with myself for letting my feelings get in the way of this friendship. This was not supposed to be my Prince Charming. I had other plans, but those darn eyes kept getting in the way!

One night, I called my sister, bawling. "I can't like him! He's a farmer, and I want to leave this town! What should I do?!" My sister's response was exactly what I needed at that moment. Immediately, I felt my spirit relax, and peace came over me when she said, "You're not marrying him tomorrow. Stop overthinking this. Relax and just have fun."

"Have fun? Relax!?" I hadn't given myself the freedom to do so in years. I had locked away my heart and constantly worried about the day someone might try to take it again. But my sister's words were like honey on my soul. I felt a newfound sense of liberation. I had spent the last few years reclaiming my heart and was now walking in the Truth. I didn't need to worry about how this relationship would unfold because God was at the center, and I had nothing to fear. I knew that regardless of whether I married him or not, this would not end the same way my previous relationship had. I had the assurance that things would be different, and I could finally experience freedom. I no longer had to keep my heart on lockdown.

After that initial wave of panic subsided and I chose to trust that God would guide this friendship, things quickly took a turn for the better! It was the kind of turn that a runner experiences at the end of a long race—a downhill stretch that feels easy and comfortable, with the wind at your back. As I ran in newfound freedom down that gentle slope, it didn't take long to catch a glimpse of the finish line. The culmination of this journey revealed a future that was unlike anything I had expected, yet it encompassed everything I had ever desired.

This is how God works: He changes our desires and blesses us with more than we can think or imagine for ourselves. Whether we live in the city or the country, these external factors don't matter when we are living the life God has called us to. I couldn't have chosen this path, but I couldn't be happier. This is the way the author of our souls operates—He grants us His best when we surrender our worst, trading our pain for freedom. All it took for me was to trust Him and His Truth, rather than relying on my feelings and this world's idea of truth.

The day I stood in the church, waiting to be walked down the aisle to become his wife, was the best day of my life. As I stood there, with my friend singing Elvis's song, 'I Can't Help Falling in Love with You,' I was completely overwhelmed with thankfulness. God had redeemed my messy story. Sobbing, I started walking down the aisle towards him, holding my dad's arm. With each step, I was engulfed by profound gratitude. I just couldn't believe how much Jesus loved me! I couldn't believe this was really happening, and I was getting to live out my dream after all my failures. As I looked ahead at my God-given groom, I cried—an ugly cry—the whole way down the aisle. I'm sure some of our guests probably wondered what was wrong with me! My most beautiful moment was met with my messiest tears! But I didn't care. At that moment, my memory was flooded with all the pains, the darkness, the loss of hope and joy. BUT in front of me, I saw Jesus's deep love and forgiveness being redeemed through that beautiful man standing there, waiting nervously to meet me at the altar.

This is the way the author of our souls operates—He grants us His best when we surrender our worst, trading our pain for freedom.

I was marrying the man of my dreams, the dream that God sorted out when I handed Him control. He was someone who loved Jesus first, respected me incessantly, understood hard work and determination, and forgave generously. Not to mention, he is incredibly nice to look at! I was bursting with gratefulness!

A MOTHER'S SUPERPOWER

Of course, my joy on this perfect day was also accompanied by a measurable amount of pain. My mother was not here; she could not share this beautiful day with us. She would have been so proud. She would have loved my man—quiet, sweet, and just the right amount of sarcastic.

Remember those poppers?

I truly believe God gave mothers a superpower when it comes to their children. That's the beautiful thing about moms; they see and know things about their children and situations unlike anyone else. She may not have known who or when I would marry, but she knew she wouldn't be there for it. Four years earlier, on the 4th of July, during that ridiculous stop at the fireworks stand, I couldn't have imagined how valuable that moment would become. She bought every case of confetti poppers they had for my wedding—this wedding. My mom was here.

Unsure if they would still work after all these years, we took our chances and let Mom's purchase be our grand finale. As we walked out of the church and our guests stood waiting, they held those poppers that my mother had purchased on her last great day, her last 4th of July with us—and at that moment, my mother played a part in my day perfectly. She knew she would not share this on the physical side but left her mark spiritually. As we exited the church and they pulled the strings, streamers rushed out and fell to the ground.

Looking around, I felt the powerful love of my mom and Jesus's unrelenting provision. Sometimes it's the simple and inexpensive things, like those champagne bottles filled with strips of paper that hold the greatest meaning in life.

Mom always knew how to throw a party, and even in her death, she made sure she didn't miss out on this one. I love that about her. Thank you, Jesus, for bringing my prince charming and for giving moms superpowers.

TO MY READERS WITHOUT A SUPERHERO MOM,

As I talk about how God gave mom's superpowers, I also understand that not all moms choose to step into that gift. Many women are too busy trying to deal and heal from their own trauma. And others think they can't surrender their lives to God.

If this is you and you lacked a superhero mom, first of all, I am sorry. The God who knit you perfectly together did not intend for it to be that way. You were created to be deeply loved and known. The good news is that you have the power to redeem that broken part of your story and to be a superhero to your own children! God is waiting to help you. You need only to ask. And trust me, this privilege is even better!

REFLECTION QUESTIONS

Food is necessary for growth. Did you ever consider the fact that we also feed our spiritual bodies? Take some time to evaluate what you are feeding yours. Where do you put your energy? Is your focus on growing through prayer, reflection, mentorship, and surrender? Or are you keeping yourself fed through making sure you are happy, taken care of, staying ahead, or looking your best? Remember: There is no shame in the development of both! The question is which one is receiving the MOST attention?

What are some areas that you have allowed your feelings to have too much authority? How can you surrender those areas to Truth?

Evaluate how much of your worth has been rooted in the approval or validation of the opposite sex. Do you need the love or affections of others to find worth in yourself? What are same steps you can take to turn your focus from that to Jesus today?

CHAPTER NINE:

Anna and Me

"*There was also a prophet, Anna, the daughter of Penuel, of the tribe of Asher. She was very old; she had lived with her husband seven years after her marriage, and then was a widow until she was eighty-four. She never left the temple but worshiped night and day, fasting and praying. Coming up to them at that very moment, she gave thanks to God and spoke about the child to all who were looking forward to the redemption of Jerusalem.*"
-Luke 2:36-38

In the previous chapter, I shared how mothers were given super-power abilities when it comes to their children. In my view, mothers possess an innate understanding of their kids that others can't comprehend, and they have a unique ability to perceive qualities that go unnoticed by most. Often, we possess a deeper knowledge of our kids than they have of themselves! It's as if God Himself winked at us from Heaven, extending His hand to give us a secret handshake.

Another way in which my mother received superpowers from God was through a letter she had written to me. Following her passing, my father began going through her belongings, and he stumbled upon a letter in her drawer that she had written to me during my high school years. It was clearly never her intention to give this letter to me while she was still alive. She had written it with her absence in mind and purposely left it at the front of her drawer for easy discovery. The letter overflowed with words of encouragement and dreams she had for me—things she saw within me and hoped I would recognize in myself. Amongst the many aspirations and desires she expressed for my future, she wrote:

"Shana, you can do anything. Of course, I believe you should be in the ministry full time, but only God can guide you in that decision."

This letter became a lifeline for me during the years following her passing, offering me tangible advice from my mother long after she had gone.

She is not the first nor the last person to have recognized a call to ministry in my life. I vividly remember one young man, during a mission trip to Europe, who declared that I had the gift of an evangelist. His words have echoed in my mind ever since. The terms "ministry" and "evangelist" have carried significant weight for me, but I have struggled to fully grasp their implications in my own life. I have never taken these declarations lightly, yet I have also grappled with understanding how they align with my path. As time passes and I grow older, I frequently find myself questioning whether I am truly fulfilling the ministry God has called me to. These introspective moments prompt me often to ask God if I am living out the purpose He has entrusted to me.

Anna the Prophetess is mentioned in three verses of the Bible. Luke introduces her when Mary and Joseph bring Jesus to the temple to offer a sacrifice in accordance with the law. Anna was incredibly old, some sources suggest she may have been as young as 84, while others propose she could have been as old as 105! Despite her age, Anna remained steadfast in her devotion. You see, she had been married for only seven years when her husband passed away, and from that point forward, she dedicated her life to worship and fasting. Considering the common practice of marrying at 15 or 16, she likely became a widow by the age of 23. From such a young age, the Bible tells us that she never left the Temple. She fasted, walked the temple, and expressed gratitude. Anna committed her life to worship, eagerly anticipating the fulfillment of the promise of a savior and waiting for decades for it to materialize. That is extraordinary patience! I can only imagine that there were moments in her life when she questioned whether this Savior she spoke of would ever come. Did she ever doubt herself or lose hope? It's likely that even others wondered if she might be mistaken in her insight! Consider the situation: someone proclaiming the arrival of the Savior at 30 years old, then 40, then 50, and still waiting at 60, 70, 80, and so on. Over time, people may have started to disregard her words or at least question them.

In my own life, I can admit that when I pray for something and it doesn't come to fruition within a few months (who am I kidding, even a few days), frustration sets in. It's easy to lose hope when prayers aren't answered within the timeline I desire. Anna, on the other hand, lived a life characterized by unwavering patience and trust. She kept her focus on the ultimate goal and had faith in God's timing. However, I also imagine that Anna had her share of challenging days. There must have been moments when God felt distant, causing her to question His plans. There were likely days when she doubted her calling and wondered if He would ever fulfill His promises. For over 80 years, she entrusted herself to God's faithfulness, patiently waiting for His word to come to pass. And then, it finally happened...

I can only imagine the day—the day she had dreamt of and talked about for years—standing right in front of her! She looked over and saw Mary and Joseph walking in with their child. This child had been the focus of her dreams for the last seven decades, and here he lay in the arms of his mother! The Bible says she immediately recognized him. What was she feeling? This day had been years in the making! Oh, what joy she must have felt! The day she had trusted would come... came! The Bible says she went straight up to them, gave thanks to God, and spoke about him being the long-awaited Savior! She had waited her whole life for this moment, and her commitment to God led her to be one of the first people to share the good news of Jesus!

Her devotion to the King led to an encounter with the Christ she had longed to see.

Anna has given me such assurance! We are never too old to be used by God, and as long as we live, He has more to teach us! In fact, He has called all of us to be ministers. God has called each of us to submit, trust, and ultimately spread the word of His great love for others!

As life marches on, many times we get wrapped up in the busyness of our day-to-day and forget the call placed on each of our lives. And some of us, pointing a finger back at myself, overthink this call. I have questioned every decision - am I walking in the call that God has on my life? Am I doing the right thing? After college, I got married and started teaching elementary school - Was that the ministry I was called to do? Then I quit teaching to raise my kids - well, certainly my family is the greatest ministry of all! Right, God? And in a blink, 20 years have passed. I have five humans that depend on me, and I have the privilege of speaking my values and hopes into them. If all else fails in this life of mine, having five people who grow into loving, Jesus-serving, hardworking members of society would be the greatest accomplishment I could ever have! Too often, parents don't see the importance of what they are doing in their home. Our society surely doesn't acknowledge it. We only see honor for the work people do outside of the home. Let me remind you, raising children matters. Remember? God made us superheroes in our homes! We have a secret handshake with God! I know, I know, most days it doesn't feel like it, but this is the backward and upside-down nature of God. He always makes beauty from our struggles. God knows raising children is the ultimate struggle! Amen?! Focusing on the people inside our homes will ultimately create the world we all want to live in. I have taken my job of raising and teaching my children very seriously. It IS my most important job, that is for sure. But I still feel Jesus whispering to me.

"There is more."

And now, here I am, a middle aged woman, and I still feel that persistent call. Do you experience a persistent pull in your life? Something you don't quite understand but cannot let go of? I was spending some time in prayer when this passage from Luke jumped off the page. It was as if God highlighted Anna's story to convey to me, 'You are not too old. I have more for you to do.' In that moment, a refreshing sense of purpose swept over me. I am living out God's calling. I am serving Him and loving my family to the best of my abilities, however, God's love for us is so immense that there is always more! Sometimes, God utilizes our age to His advantage.

Some of us require years of marinating, just like Anna. There is so much we can learn from her life. Despite losing her husband at a young age, she could have become bitter or lost all hope for her future. However, Anna chose a different path. The Bible tells us that she continually gave thanks to God day and night.

* Anna had gratitude.
* Anna was in good health. It says she fasted and walked the temple praying every day. (Mind, body and spirit- she had all parts covered.)
* She had enduring trust in God's faithfulness! It says her devotion was constant, she never gave up, she didn't let discouragement win.

And there's more...guess what Anna's name means, "favor and grace".

FAVOR.

Favor means approval. Biblically, favor brings supernatural increase, promotion, restoration, and honor. So Anna experienced supernatural increase, promotion, restoration, and honor from God. Wow! However, from an external perspective, it may not have appeared that way. She was alone, widowed at a young age, without a husband to care for her, which, in those days, was every-thing to a woman! Anna didn't seem to have favor, at least not in the way we would expect. But God's ways are different from ours. His favor and approval may look different than what we anticipate, and this can be unsettling. In fact, it probably should be. She had to trust that His ways were the best ways, despite the passing of decades and her challenging circumstances! I imagine, during the years of waiting, she sometimes questioned her favor. Much like you and I do. But God is big enough for our questions. He allows room for our doubts; we simply need to make room for Him to work through them.

GRACE.

There are two definitions of grace, and I believe both hold true in Anna's life. In the Bible, grace refers to our unmerited gift of salvation, but it also encompasses the concept of simple elegance. When I envision Anna, I see a woman of simple elegance. She embodies strength of mind and spirit, while also exuding gentleness and discernment. On difficult days, when God feels distant, and life seems to punch us in the face, we may struggle to recognize the Anna within ourselves when we look in the mirror. Elegance and favor may feel miles away! Personally, I am prone to doubts and questions when things don't go according to my plans or when prayers aren't swiftly answered. However, nobody becomes a ballerina overnight. First, we must endure the pain of bloody feet, cope with sore muscles, and battle the mental challenges that urge us to quit. Only after years of perseverance does the beautiful dance unfold!

Grace and elegance do not manifest overnight. They require a commitment to the hard work necessary to achieve them. When doubts and questions arise in my life, and impatience towards God sets in, I think of Anna. She waited her entire life for God to fulfill His promise to her. Perhaps Anna also grappled with doubts. Maybe she questioned whether God would truly fulfill what He had promised. Regardless, the Bible does not delve into her struggle; it only reveals her success. **God focuses on our triumphs!** The Bible shares the story of her beautiful dance after the toil and dedication.

The moment Anna gazed upon the baby's face, she recognized her Savior. In that instant, all the hardships and struggles of her life seemed worthwhile. Without a doubt, favor resided deep within her heart. Imagine the immense gratitude she must have felt and the overwhelming joy that accompanied God's precious gift to her! She would forever be remembered in history as the only woman named

Prophetess in the New Testament, and she would be among the first to proclaim the good news of the coming King!

BUT THERE IS EVEN MORE TO ANNA'S STORY

She hailed from the Tribe of Asher. In the book of Deuteronomy, Moses prophesied that the Tribe of Asher's "strength will equal your days." Anna lived a lengthy life, which meant she had to endure a considerable amount of time in a state of "waiting." Charles Spurgeon eloquently captures the essence of this in his sermon:

"As thy days, so shall thy strength be." It is our weakness that has made room for God to give us such a promise as this. Our sins make room for a Saviour; our frailties make room for the Holy Spirit to correct them; all our wanderings make room for the good Shepherd, that he may seek us and bring us back. We do not love nights, but we do love stars; we do not love weakness, but we do bless God for the promise that is to sustain us in our weakness, we do not admire winter, but we do admire the glittering snow; we must shudder at our own trembling weakness, but we still do bless God that we are weak because it makes room for the display of his own invincible strength in fulfilling such a promise as this."

C. SPURGEON

Some of us need more time before we are ready to step into the fullness of God's call for us. Everything we do in life is part of this plan. Every difficult circumstance we encounter pushes us towards growth and guides us into maturity. We don't love pain, but we appreciate what we learn from it when we allow God to step into our pain with us. We don't love waiting, but we can appreciate what waiting produces in our lives if we let God be the cultivator of that waiting. Anna can teach us so much about how God's ways are different from ours, but always better! I am going to lean into my inner Anna, focusing more on doing my job of trusting, waiting, praying, fasting, walking

Every difficult circumstance
we encounter pushes us
towards growth and guides
us into maturity.

We don't love pain, but we
appreciate what we learn from
it when we allow God to step
into our pain with us. We
don't love waiting, but we can
appreciate what waiting produces
in our lives if we let God be the
cultivator of that waiting.

(I better keep those legs moving so God can use me when I am old!), and giving thanks for who He is today!

In God's perfect timing, He will fulfill my calling according to His plan, not mine. And He will do the same for you! Let's embrace gratitude in the everyday, even in the mundane, the mundane is part of our calling! Trust in the waiting, the waiting is part of our calling. And let's learn to recognize Jesus walking beside us along the way. Our ministry has already begun; just take a look around.

REFLECTION QUESTIONS:

Maybe you're like me, and have often questioned the call of God on your life. Have you felt frustrated or questioned if you are doing the right thing? What if we changed the way we viewed our calling? What if our calling was marked by our preparation. Are you living out calling on your life today? Are you expecting, trusting, and preparing as if God's calling is actively taking place? OR are you living in the question, allowing doubt and frustration to rise up?

What if we lived each day, even the mundane, "called"? What would that look like? How would that change your day to day?

What are some action steps you can take to actively walk towards God's purpose for your life? Maybe you need to spend more quiet time with Him? Maybe you need to get more exercise to keep your body young? Look around, what are some things you can change?

CHAPTER TEN:

Exposing the Lies

*"Be careful with your thoughts because
your thoughts become your words.*

*Be careful with your words because
your words become your actions.*

*Be careful with your actions because
your actions become your character.*

*And be careful with your character because
your character becomes your destination."*

-Lao-Tze

What is your desired destination? What are your dreams and plans for your future? Have you considered the importance of your thoughts in achieving these goals? Many of us tend to treat our thought life as something that simply happens, without realizing that we have the power to control it. When we allow our minds to wander freely without any reins, it can hinder God's good plan for our lives. Unfortunately, this kind of feeling-centered living is common these days. It was my uncontrolled thoughts that led to poor choices and took more from me than I ever anticipated giving up. However, the good news is that we can change this pattern. We can learn how to take captive every thought and make it obedient to Christ. While obedience may not be glorified in our culture, it is through this obedience that we can find our most fulfilling future. By doing so, we can reach the destination we have always dreamed of having!

God has crafted our bodies in a truly remarkable way! We are intricately designed and composed of three essential components: body, spirit, and soul. In the previous chapter, we explored how Anna embodied the ideal balance in maintaining the well-being of these three parts. Each component holds equal significance and requires nurturing for us to lead our most fulfilling lives. If just one area is neglected, all the other areas will suffer.

Our body is the easiest to understand, the most visible, and the part we naturally take care of best. It serves as our house, housing our spirit and soul. However, our body is the only aspect of ourselves that is temporary. Although it is our responsibility to nurture it as best we can, the body will ultimately die. Nevertheless, it remains crucial to prioritize good nutrition, exercise, rest, and kindness towards our bodies, as a healthy body facilitates the cultivation of a healthy spirit and soul.

Our spirit is the element of our being that establishes a connection and facilitates communication with God. It is an inner space that yearns to be filled. When we experience salvation, God fills that void with the Holy Spirit. In Greek, the word "pneuma" can be translated as "spirit," "breath," or "unseen force." Following Jesus' departure from Earth, God bestowed upon us the Holy Spirit, which represents His own spirit, His breath, and this is undoubtedly the greatest gift of all.

> *"But the Advocate, the Holy Spirit, whom the Father will send in my name, will teach you all things and will remind you of everything I have said to you."*

JOHN 14:26

The Bible is very clear that we must seek this gift through salvation and dedication to Jesus. If we don't ask for salvation through Christ, we will not experience the filling of the Holy Spirit. **God's breath will not be within us.**

> *"If you love me, keep my commands. And I will ask the Father, and he will give you another advocate to help you and be with you forever - the Spirit of truth. The world cannot accept him, because it neither sees him nor knows him. But you know him, for he lives with you and will be in you."*

JOHN 14:15-17

It is crucial to be filled with the Holy Spirit as it empowers us, grants us wisdom, discernment, and spiritual authority. God, as our helper and guide, equips us through His Spirit. When we lack the presence of the Holy Spirit, the gods of this world can blind the minds of unbelievers, leading to confusion dominating our thoughts and hearts. Rest assured, the space within us will be filled with something! However, we can choose to fill it with the Truth, and the only way to do so is by embracing God's Truth—the Holy Spirit.

"In their case the god of this world has blinded the minds of the unbelievers, to keep them from seeing the light of the gospel of the glory of Christ, who is the image of God."

2 CORINTHIANS 4:4

God makes it so easy for us. We only need to ask Him to fill that space with His Holy Spirit.

His spirit will help us see Truth.

The most complex aspect of our being is **our soul.** The soul has three components: our thoughts, our will, and our emotions. Many of my failures can be traced back to these areas. I did not fully comprehend the immense power they held. Moreover, I failed to realize that, in Christ, I possessed the authority to control them. God designed us to experience a wide range of emotions, and often we assign value to them. We tend to label happiness as good and jealousy as bad. However, why would God create negative emotions? The truth is, He didn't. The Bible reveals that God is a jealous God and even experiences anger. Our feelings themselves are neither good nor bad; rather, they serve as indicators of what is happening within us. For much of my life, I attached excessive importance to each feeling I had. Instead, emotions can act as helpful signals, pointing us toward areas that require examination, consideration, and often healing. For instance, if I enter a room filled with people but feel isolated and unaccepted, I should ask myself, "Why do I feel this way? Where is this sentiment coming from?" rather than accepting that feeling as truth, we should inquire into its origins. Unfortunately, we often choose the latter approach, leading us to mistakenly conclude that we are indeed alone, when in reality, this is not the case. By paying attention to our emotions and posing thoughtful questions about them, we can embark on a journey of transformation. Curiosity regarding the reasons behind our emotions and their sources can pave the way for personal growth.

Most importantly, we must avoid being carried away by our emotions. If we picture our feelings like boats sailing down a fast-flowing river, we do not have to impulsively hop aboard. **We always have a choice.** We can remain on the riverbank, observing the boats (feelings) as they pass, or we can choose to jump aboard. We can acknowledge our feelings and allow curiosity to guide us, or we can yield to the emotions and allow them to sail us away. The authority lies in our hands. Remember, feelings themselves are neither inherently good nor bad. They lack moral value and are not right or wrong. **They do not represent truth,** nor should they dictate how we lead our lives. You need not be swept downstream; you can stand on solid ground.

During my formative years, a significant portion of my life was governed by the influence of my thoughts and feelings. Regrettably, rather than critically evaluating my emotions, I naively accepted them as truth. I think this is often the case in our youth. And it's the responsibility of us parents to teach our kids otherwise. I mistakenly believed that every mistake I made defined me as a failure. Additionally, I fell victim to lies whispered in my ear. Did I experience failures? Yes, without a doubt. However, it is important to note that those failures did not make me a failure as a person. Instead of embracing these thoughts and emotions and allowing them to steer me off course, I could have chosen a different approach. I could have fostered curiosity and posed intro-

Emotions can act as helpful signals, pointing us toward areas that require examination, consideration, and often healing.

spective questions. Why did I anchor my sense of worth solely in my behavior? What led me to believe that a life free from mistakes was the only path to attaining worthiness?

How about you? Where is your sense of worthiness rooted? Do you find yourself believing that you must meet certain behavioral standards in order to be loved? Perhaps you have also viewed your feelings as truth, allowing them to carry you away. Regardless, what truly matters is recognizing these feelings for what they are, acknowledging their presence, and posing insightful questions about them. Whatever you do, resist the temptation to get on that boat!

Fixating on negative thoughts is similar to navigating a deep river that relentlessly pulls us in that direction, carving and contorting our mental current.

Often, we are quick to recognize when a thought is unhealthy or unproductive. We can sense when we are generating pain within our own minds. However, actually expelling these thoughts is another challenge altogether. It is difficult because these thoughts often feel undeniably true. Sometimes, it may even feel comforting to allow negative thoughts to linger and permeate our consciousness. These thoughts have a tendency to cling to us, reluctant to leave. As we entertain and indulge in these thoughts, they begin to forge pathways within our minds (neural pathways). These pathways resemble deep trenches, and the more we persist in thinking a certain way, the more pronounced these grooves become. Fixating on negative thoughts is similar to navigating a deep river that relentlessly pulls us in that direction, carving and contorting our mental current.

"Finally, brothers, whatever is true, whatever is honorable, whatever is just, whatever is pure,

whatever is lovely, whatever is commendable, if there is any excellence, if there is anything worthy of praise, think about these things."

PHILIPPIANS 4:8

While working on the chapter about believing and listening to lies, I found myself unexpectedly falling into a deep pit of them. Feelings of failure, inadequacy, unworthiness, and fear anchored themselves and refused to let go. Despite praying, shedding tears, and attempting to reason myself out of the turmoil, it seemed as if nothing was making a difference. **However, while I prayed, I continued to allow myself to be carried down the raging river of negative thinking.** In some ways, it felt like a safe haven, shielding me from potential harm and vulnerability. However, when the mind becomes entangled, the body inevitably follows suit. I found myself, struggling to get out of bed in the mornings and lacking the motivation to carry on with normal tasks. I felt like a failure, consumed by discouragement that robbed me of both joy and productivity. Its effects permeated all aspects of my life.

This is an experience that can happen to anyone. Do you loath exercise? Are you unwittingly carving deep trenches of dread when you contemplate the effort required to improve your health? If so, you must get out of the boat! Are you trapped in a toxic relationship? Similar to my experience, you may have sailed away with the belief that this is your only option and that you don't deserve any better. Again, get out. Don't spend another second sailing down that river. Do you repeatedly tell yourself that you don't belong or that something in your life will never change? You've got to stop letting the current pull you downstream!

This tendency to dwell on negativity is something we should

anticipate. Our adversaries patiently wait for an opportunity to derail us. They are well aware of our vulnerabilities and insecurities. For example, have you ever experienced an incredible day? A day where everything seems to be going smoothly, the kids are getting along, and everyone is accomplishing their tasks with minimal complaints or effort? During these moments, you feel like you're excelling in life! Your parenting skills are on point, and you believe your children are destined for greatness! But then, the next day arrives... oh, that dreaded next day. Reality hits hard, and everything falls apart. Nobody listens, everyone is bickering, the house is a mess and you can't even gather yourself enough to brush your hair, let alone prepare a meal! I've noticed that often, our good days are swiftly followed by bad ones. But don't entertain those negative thoughts! Even on your worst day, you're still doing an amazing job. You're not failing. Don't let your adversary throw you off course! And who needs a clean house or brushed hair, anyway?

If we embark on the journey of creating new healthy neural pathways in our brains, healing from past wounds, and assisting others through our experiences, **we should be prepared for challenges in those very areas.** It is quite common that just when we believe we have triumphed over a significant obstacle in our lives, we are reminded that there are always more obstacles. Our journey towards fulfillment will only be reached when we enter the gates of heaven!

"Blessed is the one who perseveres under trial because, having stood the test, that person will receive the crown of life that the Lord has promised to those who love him."

JAMES 1:12

If you're similar to me, there are occasions when I find myself spiraling into self-deprecation rapidly and unexpectedly, only realizing it once it has already taken its toll. It feels undeniably real and overwhelming. This is precisely why the Bible instructs us to remain vigilant at all times. God comprehends our nature so deeply! He understands that we easily succumb to negative thoughts and that the adversary of our minds eagerly seeks to consume us. Thankfully, He has equipped us with all the necessary tools to overcome the enemy within our thoughts- through reading the Bible, prayer, and confession (be it a friend or professional)- but it is our responsibility to apply them!

Be alert and of sober mind. Your enemy the devil prowls around like a roaring lion looking for someone to devour.

1 PETER 5:8

God's mercies are new each day! You see, sometimes we need to be reminded that we have already won. We are already victorious with Jesus! We don't need to worry or fear tomorrow because when our hope and joy are in Him, we have nothing to fear.

"Put on the full armor of God, so that you can take your stand against the devil's schemes. For our struggle is not against flesh and blood, but against the rulers, against the authorities, against the powers of this dark world and against the spiritual forces of evil in the heavenly realms."

EPHESIANS 6:11-12

Does God speak to us? If He's the God I read about in the Bible, then of course! So why is it so hard to hear Him? And often, even harder to obey. How do we discern the voice of God? How do we differentiate where these thoughts are coming from? I often question the ideas and thoughts in my head. Was that God? Was that me? It just doesn't seem that obvious! If these thoughts push me out of my comfort zone and lead me towards something that aligns with God's word, then it could quite possibly be God. However, if we continually dismiss these thoughts because they feel too scary or intimidating, it will become increasingly harder to hear His voice.

Think about it. If you try to talk to someone and they continually dismiss you, you will stop talking to them! If you feel like God is asking something of you and you keep ignoring it, He will stop talking too. If God tries to communicate with us and we doubt and choose not to listen, soon we will not be able to recognize His voice. Maybe, just maybe, if we actually started living out these God-given thoughts, denying fear and insecurity control, we would slowly and steadily start to recognize His voice with certainty.

Over and over again in the Bible, God requires action steps on our part first and then He moves. Our obedience is a necessary part of our relationship with Him. In James 4:7-10 God requires our action! **Submit, come near to God** then God will come near to you, **wash** your hands, **purify** your hearts, **grieve, mourn, wail,** and **humble** yourselves then he will lift you up. Action steps from us first and then, God works. In James 2:17 it reminds us that faith without action is dead.

In the United States, there are very few situations where obedience is absolutely necessary. We have become accustomed to bending rules, doing our own thing, and living comfortably with minimal consequences. We tend to avoid discomfort and resist situations where we feel a loss of control. However, living for Jesus should involve relinquishing control and embracing challenges. The question arises: If our primary goal in life is to be free from discomfort (which, if we're honest, is the case for most of us), can we truly claim to live a surrendered life?

It's true that God uses not only our actions but also our insecurities to stretch us and prompt us to step out in faith. If we struggle with concerns about what others think of us, that's precisely where God will challenge us to take action. If fear is an area of struggle, we can be sure that God will require us to move forward despite it. And even in moments of doubt, God will stretch our faith in various ways. His love for us is so immense that He doesn't want us to remain stagnant; He desires and requires our growth. Growth happens through stretching, which can be uncomfortable, just like the pains experienced during physical growth in our childhood. Although growing pains may not feel pleasant, they contribute to our height, something everyone desires. Likewise, we don't want to remain weak-minded. Therefore, we should anticipate experiencing some growing pains in our thoughts as well. God's work of growth within us may cause discomfort, but it is through this discomfort that we are pushed to evolve.

The sooner we become comfortable with a little discomfort, the faster we will experience growth.

The next time you have a thought, any thought, ask yourself some questions about it. What does the Bible say about this? Does it align with how Christ lived? Will this stretch and grow me? Does it challenge me? Will this have the potential to positively impact others? Is this thought true? If the thought is negative, get rid of it! You know where it came from, and we aren't listening to that voice anymore! However, if the thought aligns with scripture, step out! Trust that the God who made all things is speaking to you. Take a chance and see what happens. Come with expectation and act in obedience. **Be brave! Grow that courage muscle!** This is where all the goodness starts. And this is how we learn to recognize His voice!

Let's think way back to the beginning of this book. Do you remember how I talked about the cost of living? Every choice has a price tag and we get to choose where we put our "money".

* Doing the right thing is hard. Doing the wrong thing is hard.
* Earning money is hard. Being broke is hard.
* Finding good friends is hard. Living with lousy ones is hard.
* Getting healthy is hard. Being unhealthy is also hard.
* Saving yourself for one man is hard. Losing yourself to many is hard.
* Trusting God is hard. Trusting the world is hard.
* Choose your hard.

Each choice we make will cost us. Each choice starts with a thought. Each thought is rooted in lies or Truth. Who is on the throne in your mind? And what exactly do you believe?

Nothing in life is free, but we have been given the power to live a life that is infused with God's goodness! Embrace that opportunity! God has granted us the freedom to choose. All we need to do is ask! With the creator of the universe on our side, we have nothing to fear and everything to gain when we exercise our God-given authority. Remember, you are not defined by your failures- cut those ties. You are not controlled by your emotions- get off that boat. You are a cherished child of the King, and He has magnificent plans for you if you place your trust in His ways.

Thank you for taking this journey with me. To close, I would like to pray with you:

Lord,

Thank you for helping me have the courage to trust in you. I pray that my friends who are reading this will be filled with Godly courage as these words resonate in their minds. May you guide them in lifting the veil between the physical and spiritual realms, enabling them to perceive reality as it truly is. Help them to take a firm stance on the side of the Creator and to live boldly in the Truth. Expose the lies they have been believing in their own lives and wrap your loving arms around them today. We are grateful for your unwavering love for us. Thank you for using all of our failures to lead us into lasting freedom. Be King of my heart and Lord of my life.

Amen

Now, go and shine brightly! May God himself, the God of peace, sanctify you through and through. May your whole spirit, soul and body be kept blameless at the coming of our Lord Jesus Christ. The one who calls you is faithful and He will do it! Go be the person God has destined you to be—an over-comer. The power to overcome is already in you, you need only to strengthen that muscle! Thank you for taking this journey with me. I love you.

Your friend and sister in Christ,

-Shana

"Now may the God of peace himself sanctify you completely, and may your whole spirit and soul and body be kept blameless at the coming of our Lord Jesus Christ. He who calls you is faithful; he will surely do it."

1 THESSALONIANS 5:23-24

About the Author

Shana Peltz is a wife, a mother to 5 kiddos and a bonus child, a friend, a teacher of fitness and school, but most importantly a follower of Jesus. Passionate about sunshine, coffee, good conversations, music, traveling, fitness, and discovering truth. Shana was a public school teacher turned homeschool enthusiast, who loves helping moms settle into their God-given destiny. Born and raised in Bismarck, North Dakota.